Five-Star Sundays, Two-Star Mondays

(An Un-Altar-ed Memoir by a minister's daughter)

LAIRD T. WHITE

I dedicate this book to all the beloved members of
my family: my husband, my children, my grandchildren
and my slew of nieces and nephews.

CONTENTS

acknowledgements

Thanks to my editor, Laura Didyk; to my very observant
proof reader, Sharon Palma and my talented designer,
Lisa Cavender. Cover photo by Reid White... circa 3,000 BC

Smoke gets in thine eyes

1 HOLY SMOKE

It is 11:30 on a Sunday morning in May and my father is in the middle of delivering his sermon at St. Peter's Episcopal Church in Morristown, New Jersey. I, the youngest daughter of four children, consider St. Peter's "Daddy's church," even though he has only preached here for the last year and a half. In my eleven-year-old mind, the impressive stature of St. Peter's is nothing in comparison to my six-foot father, or to his sermons. St. Peter's is lofty and formal. My father, and his sermons, are down-to-earth, and sometimes peppered with humor.

This Sunday, my mother, two sisters, my brother and I are seated in our regular pew, three rows back from the front row where the minister's family usually sits because this is as close to the front pew as Mother can bear. As always, she sits smack at the row's end next to the aisle. She sits here because of her so-called "claustrophobia," a word I later come to recognize as code for her being a closet Unitarian. Beneath her proper minister's-wife façade, I know she's thinking about the new shoes she just bought.

The church is filled, front to back, but there is very little noise considering the size of the congregation. There are no babies crying, for this is the '40s when babies are not well-known in public. Only the usual shifting of feet, the occasional cough or rustling of prayer books and hymnals can be heard along with my father's voice. The sun streams down through the stained glass windows onto clouds of dust motes, turning them into shafts of heavenly golden sparkles. Wafting through the church are familiar smells of wood wax, brass polish, scented hankies, shined-up-shoes, paraffin, and altar flowers. All of these effusions get caught up in Mother's perfume, "L'Heure Bleu," the only perfume she will ever use. I have never smelled this distinctive perfume on any other mothers—theirs are sweet-smelling— but this fragrance is as sharp as pine needles.

Despite the limitations of a minister's salary, Mother does everything to perfection. She makes most of her clothes and all of ours and keeps our home—the very large rectory, which she has deemed, 'The Episcopal Palace"— in tip-top condition. She gets her decorating ideas from House Beautiful and, somewhere, has learned the arts of reupholstering, laying carpet, and wallpapering. Her in-town gardens are outstanding, and she will soon become president of the local garden club.

Mother is not above a prankish sense of humor. She is also not above bouts of sadness followed by spurts of whirlwind energy during which she'll paint two rooms, make curtains for my room and refinish two bureaus, all in one week! What she fears most are what she calls "Church Do's," those functions that entail giving teas to vestry women, attending church picnics, altar guild meetings, hosting visiting bishops, and being present, in her pew, always on view, at every service. She tells us she would prefer to pray alone, "thank you!," but being the minister's wife and a "preacher's kid" herself, she does the right thing, so here she is again at St. Peter's this Sunday, with her kids spruced-up and in tow.

This morning, my sisters and I are in our summer straw hats, white cotton gloves, clutching the brand new patent leather pocketbooks Mother bought us for Easter. My oldest sister, Anne, wears a dove-gray suit and sits casually by me with one very long silky leg crossed over and wrapped around the other. She works at Scribner's Bookstore in New York City and reminds me of Lauren Bacall. I have been trying to imitate her leg-wrap for months, but being nine years younger, can't make it work, and in short white socks it would look ridiculous.

Rob, my fourteen-year-old brother, is wearing his Sunday "real" clothes—a seersucker suit and tie—and sits next to Mother. Next to him is my other sister, Sally, sitting with her back as straight as an arrow. She is seventeen and the female athlete of the family. She is a terrific tennis player and diver and when I see a Superwoman cartoon, I think of Sal. When she's home from boarding school and if I've had a bad dream, she is the one who sleeps in my room and talks me out of the dark.

Mother is wearing her beige linen suit, copied from a

McCall's pattern stitched on her Singer sewing machine late at night. Today, she wears a white shell pin on her lapel, which nicely echoes her snappy white hat with the veil that comes across her Claudette Colbert cheekbones and halfway down her chin. She is now engrossed with Dad's words and stares up at him in the pulpit. He is handsome in his robes, and her slightly slanted eyes are transfixed with interest. Maybe she is planning tomorrow's dinner, or a murder—one never knows with Mother— but it is clear to anyone looking at her that she, the devoted wife, is totally absorbed.

Daddy is speaking about the Pharisees, a subject dear to his nonpolitical, "low-church" soul. We kids adore the nonbelieving, cruel Pharisees because they are true villains in the Great Jesus Mystery and, according to Daddy, there are many still out there. When preaching about the lesson of "Do Unto Others," he would give his congregation real-life examples of how giving and kind treatment can benefit others.

We also love Daddy's voice, especially when he reads Dickens or The Saturday Evening Post to us during our summer vacations in New Hampshire. His voice is like Gregory Peck's, deeply resonant, and being a natural actor he instinctively knows how to deliver a sermon with care and good timing. He could be reading a shopping list, a batting lineup, or the newspaper "funnies" and his congregation would be entranced.

At this moment, out of the corner of my eye, I see a slight movement from where Mother sits, followed by a tiny snapping sound. I look down the pew and see Mother's hand, as if in slow motion, emerging from her pocketbook, her long Revlon-tipped fingers folded around a cigarette and her ever-present Zippo lighter. Helpless and horrified I watch her hand arc toward her mouth, where, with the finesse of a surgeon, she inserts the cigarette cleanly, miraculously, through a hole in her 1940's veil, flips her Zippo, and God, help us—lights up. She smokes so often that she's totally unaware of what she's doing.

My brother, who has been ogling a pretty blonde in the choir stalls, realizes what's happened, but only after Mother has inhaled deeply and blown a heavy plume of smoke straight up into the air as truck drivers do in the movies. With the speed of a snake's tongue, Rob's arm shoots out and he grabs her cigarette, crushes it under his shoe and puts the butt in his pocket. But it is too late. A white cloud hangs over Mother's head and begins curling its way up to the church dome above. Soon the acrid smell of smoke is everywhere. All around me I hear tiny gasps of horror; little snickers of laughter. I can even hear them coming from the choir loft above the entrance to the church. Realizing what she's done, Mother looks down the pew at us, crosses her eyes, squinches her lips into a figure eight, and then wiggles them up and down. This is her famous "fish face," something she does when she feels she's overshot her boundaries or when we children plead for her to do it. We love this face. It is Mother at her best.

The "fish face" takes only a second and then Mother casually slides her left arm along the back of the pew behind Rob. This is her signal that the show is over and that there will be no uncontrollable, spasmodic "church giggles", as she calls them. I can see a slight "Who, me?" expression on her face as she looks up at Daddy who has seen everything, but with the help of God, has maintained his equanimity and somehow is still speaking. He lowers his half-glasses over his nose and peers down like an old dog observing a naughty puppy, but there is a slight upturn to his lips. What Mother has done is so bad that it's funny.

In these few seconds we, the children of Dad, "our God-speaker," have united into an army that must fight our enemies—those giggles. We've become entranced with our shoes, as if they've suddenly turned to gold. I breathe deeply, like I do at the doctor's office, and think of hideous things: decapitations; disembowelments, starving Armenians and polio. Anything to prevent spurts of laughter.

Staring at my navy-blue shoes with the button straps, I sneak a peek at my new Gardner watch and count the minutes until the recessional. I calculate about fifteen minutes before I am reprieved and can trail behind my family down the aisle with my best friend, Mary Treat Nettleton, to the freedom of outside. There, she and I will edge our way from the line of adults shaking hands with my father and race to the adjacent graveyard that lies between the church and my rectory home. There among the lilies of the valley and the slabs of death, we will clasp each other and howl with laughter until the tears run. Mary Treat will ask me if I'm shocked at my mother's behavior and I'll say, "You never know with Mother." Deep down I'm thrilled that Mother made this historic, hysterical mistake, and best of all, made it in church!!

Later that afternoon, I will record all of this on the special blank pages in the back of my small leather diary. My entry will be written in big red letters, underlined and surrounded with a marquee of stars, crayoned in gold. It says, "Five-Star Sunday!! Mother Smokes in Church!!! Holy Smoke!!"

Dressed for elevation   *Dressed for revelation*

2 FROM THE ALPS TO THE APSE

Although Dad spent a lot of time preaching, he never preached at home—he left that to Mother. I remember one thundery night when Mother was away and I was the only child at home. I was hiding under my covers when, suddenly, I heard a knock on the door. Dad came in and said, "Laird. It's scary out there, isn't it?"

I came out from under the covers, whispered, "Yes," and he took me to his room, let me snuggle under his covers and read Mary Poppins to me until I fell asleep. At other times, if I was sitting with grownups, knowing that I must be quiet, he would pull the sleeve of his jacket down over his hand, stick out one finger, wiggle it at me and make a little squeak, like a mouse. He'd wink and, no longer feeling alone, I'd laugh. Dad's empathy extended into his life as a minister. His sermons were centered around his belief that God is in all of us and, if sought, will lead us down paths of goodness to higher ground. Kindness was inherent in Dad and the main trait that led him up the long path to the pulpit.

Dad was born in 1898 and in his early childhood lived in Astoria, New York. When he finally became a minister, he used to joke that the reason he became one was because he was born next to hell—the nearby area called Hell's Kitchen which, at that time, was home to Irish members of the working class. Because of an ancient, blood-connect to Constantine he was given the Roman name of Cornelius Polhemus Trowbridge and the fact that his father's first name was Augustus, always made me imagine them dressed in togas, sitting in the Roman Coliseum while Stewart Granger raced his chariot around the arena, fighting off the evil gladiators. To those who knew him well, he was "Corny"—and he often was.

His parents were totally opposite in their views of religion. His father was an atheist physicist, his mother, Sarah, a rigid Episcopalian and a minister's child. The fact that a very religious woman had married an atheist scientist was a mystery to many. Granny T. (as we called her) was tall, beautiful, socially entertaining, and had a very quick mind. She not only worshiped God, she worshiped good behavior. During Prohibition she went into New York City, stood on bars, and with her classy legs peeking from under her ankle-length skirt, preached against what was then called "Jass music"—in her mind a sin. Her relationship with her children was a formal one. She required them to go to church, be polite and study hard, but it was Dad's father—despite his atheistic views—who influenced Dad's life the most. He was the brilliant, physicist parent who "made news" but, also, the one who carried the humor gene and made life—fun.

During Prohibition, which started on July 31, 1930— (known as the "thirsty first" of July)—"Father T." figured out a way to make bathtub gin by mathematically tweaking the proscribed formula of distillation. It was still gin made in a bathtub but it was made differently than specified in the law banning it. Needless to say, his parties were famously well attended. One oft-told story has him standing on a podium at Princeton, ready to hand out diplomas to his graduate students. One young man weaves his way up the aisle, obviously drunk. The crowd of on-lookers hushes in anticipation of how Professor Trowbridge will handle this dicey situation. The boy makes it up the stairs to the dais. Father T. hands him his diploma, lowers his glasses and whispers loudly into the microphone, "Was it MINE?" The boy collapses onto his chair and the audience collapses with laughter—everyone knew of Father T.'s bathtub supply.

Another famous story had to do with a robbery that took place in his home when Sarah's jewelry was stolen. This experience gave Father T. occasion to observe professional detectives in action. The robber wasn't found, but not long after the robbery there was an outbreak of thefts of radio equipment from Princeton's Palmer Laboratory research rooms. A local boy—a punk—was suspected and several times questioned, but without results. Father T. knew the detectives involved and asked them to give him five minutes alone with the boy, during which time he got a confession, resulting in the return of the stolen property. When asked how he had induced the boy to confess, Father T. replied, "You fellows don't talk this boy's language, so I just talked like a dick to the boy and said as gruffly as I could: 'Come on now—can the guff! Ya better spill the game. Ya done it and ya know ya done it.' The boy came right out with it."

By this time, Father T. had worked his way up to being dean of Princeton's graduate school. He was noted for his work inspiring new students to pursue their interests without having to immediately decide their future goals, thereby allowing them freedom to change from one chosen major to another, a choice not given by other universities. But his most known achievement was his scientific contributions during WWI.

As a young man, Father T. had studied in Germany and while at Princeton, he took many pre-war trips to Germany where he met with other scientists and worked on experiments having to do with defense mechanisms. It was during this time that he set up what was called the Sound and Flash Ranging Service for the American Forces. He discovered how an infantry unit could tell the distance between their unit and the enemy's by the electrical and radioactive proponents in the waves of distant sounds of gunshots. Because of this he was made Lt. Colonel and because of his work, which was utilized in WWI, he won many important medals of honor, including a

Distinguished Service medal and France's Officier de la Legion d'Honneur. His scientific mind also led him to—not a theory pertaining to war, but a theory of the existence of—ghosts.

While on a trip to Europe, he and Granny T. went to Italy, and during their travels, visited an historic Italian villa. Father T. went into the villa with the tour guide while Granny T. sat on an ancient stone bench outside, gazing at the beautiful old courtyard. Suddenly, the tour guide and Father T. heard loud screaming and rushed outside to see the cause. Granny T. was pointing to an empty area of the courtyard screaming "Stop those men! They're going to kill each other!" (Granny T., the ultimate "lady," was not the kind to scream or act up in any way). After a while, Father T. was able to calm her down and get her to describe what she saw—two men dressed in medieval clothes fighting with swords. The guide, in shock, said, "I was just going to show you the written history of a famous duel between the villa's owner and a rival landowner and how the owner had been killed. Your wife was pointing to the exact spot where this duel happened! Even her description of their clothes fits what they would have been wearing!" Father T.'s theory of this happening was that at times of extreme stress, we all give off waves of electricity—(ions)—and when this happens these electric ions are so strong that they are picked up and absorbed in nearby solid objects, such as the stone bench where Granny T. had been sitting. His theory was that if someone who has even a small part of that ionic makeup comes near the solid object, that person is able, by means of the meshing of these ions, to see an image of the person, or persons, who emitted the waves of electricity. To Father T. it was obvious that his wife had similar ions to the ones in the stone bench, which allowed her to see the duel fought a century before. Whether you buy it or not, this story shows Father T.'s belief that all things are related in some way to the realm of science.

I regret that I never knew my grandfather. He died before I was born. I would like to have known his scientific mind. Years ago, I found some of his letters in one of Mother's trunks that are stored in my attic. When Father T. became old and was losing his health, he and his wife spent their last days together in their beloved France. Two weeks before his death, he wrote a scientific argument about the possibility of an afterlife. In the letter there is one sentence that says it all: "The second possibility is the orthodox Christian belief that when a physical being of blood, bone and muscle is conceived, there is created a spiritual entity which accompanies the physical body through life and that, after death persists . . . This possibility would seem, both from the philosophic and from the present day scientific point of view, utterly untenable."

Apparently, his sons didn't think a spiritual entity utterly untenable, as they both became ministers. Dad, however, took the longest to reach that occupation. Not religious when he was young, Dad's loves were "whooping it up," especially in the Princeton Triangle Club (which to this day puts on musicals) and the revered, snobby Ivy Club. Being handsome, with dark hair and a straight Roman nose to go with his lofty Roman name—he fit right in. When not having mountains of fun, Dad climbed mountains *for* fun.

Dad spent many summers with his family in the Adirondacks where he developed his first love of climbing and, when he was fifteen, over in Italy with his parents, he climbed Monte Rosa with two other men in his group. His sister, Katherine, an accomplished climber herself, came along. Monte Rosa is over fifteen thousand feet but in his memoir, Dad writes, "there was nothing difficult or dangerous about the climb." Really? One of the men on the climb suffered rapid heart palpitations while climbing. As he lay there "resting" he looked overhead and saw an inscription which read: "On this spot the Duke d'Abbruzzi perished in the first attempt to ascend this mountain." Immediately, the man got to his feet and finished the climb. On returning to their hotel, Dad discovered that Katherine had made the ascent with a badly swollen leg, causing extreme pain at every step. She'd been roped to Dad and their guide, but neither had been aware of her ordeal. Sadly, during the beginning of WWI, Katherine, while helping wounded soldiers disembark from ships landing in Manhattan, died of influenza—the disease which killed more American soldiers and civilians than the Germans. The family never fully recovered from her death. In his memoir, Dad writes that while suffering the loss of his sister, he learned for the first time "how friends and their love bring strength to the suffering," an important first step in Dad's climb to the ministry.

Dad's love of mountain climbing lasted for years. When he was twenty-four years old, he climbed three more mountains in the Alps near the valley of Zermatt. Climbing never stopped. When visiting some friends in Dublin, New Hampshire, he climbed Mount Monadnock that, years later, we would be able to see from "Green Pastures", our New

Hampshire summer home. One time, in late fall, a blizzard struck suddenly and one of his best friends was killed while climbing the mountain. Thankfully, this tragic happening did not stop Dad's climbing career. I remember him once saying that as he got older, climbing and looking at the beauty above and below made him feel closer to God.

Before Dad entered Princeton in 1917, he wanted to go into the service as soon as possible but, as the age for commissions had been lowered from age twenty-one to eighteen, he just missed it and instead, he said, he was given the rank of "shave tail" in the infantry. Instead of being shipped to France—which he wanted—he went to various colleges to train younger boys who were enlisted in Student's Army Training. He also did volunteer work.

One time when the firemen of the Pennsylvania Railroad went on strike, resulting in a lack of milk for the children of New York City, Princeton students were asked to be "scabs," (those who refused to strike) by taking over for the strikers and run the trains for which they would earn some money. Two students were assigned to each engine. They slept in the railroad's YMCA, shoveled coal, and risked the dangerous, slippery steps between each moving car. The strike lasted a week. Afterward, Dad suggested he and his fellow scabs give their money to a fund for striker's families, but he was shouted down. He writes, "I learned how hard it is for Idealism to win out over Materialism."

That same summer he had an experience that strongly affected his view of how to live life. He met the very respected Dr. Wilfred Grenfell, who, when a young medical student in England, had discovered that there were groups of English immigrants living on the coast of Labrador, suffering very hard lives without medical services. So, instead of becoming a Harley Street Specialist, he single-handedly started a medical mission to help. Admiring and liking Dr. Grenfell, Dad sailed to Labrador and became a volunteer worker for the Grenfell Mission. The Mission had started its work in 1893 when Grenfell recruited two nurses and two doctors and later opened cottage hospitals along the coast of Labrador. Although originally founded to serve the local area, the mission widened to include the aboriginal peoples and settlers along the coasts of Labrador, as well as the eastern side of the peninsula of northern Newfoundland. Dr. Grenfell was later knighted for his years of service on behalf of the people of these communities. During his summer at the Grenfell Mission, Dad had one very unusual day when *he* didn't offer his services—but someone else did!

A local fur trader had offered to take him across the straits of St. Anthony to see some friends, but the night before, a strong storm struck out at sea and they were unable to go. However, out in the calmer harbor there was a fishing boat with a crew of one man and his daughter. The fur trader knew the fisherman and so he and Dad risked the waves to go out to the boat for a visit. The young girl and her father were fun to be with and drinks were served all around. After dinner, the girl—with her father's consent— made it known that she'd like to sleep with the "young Yank." For Dad—the well-raised son of a devout, Christian mother—this was definitely a "no no." Dad writes, "Rightly or wrongly, I didn't accept the invitation." This was the only time he'd been directly solicited until he was in his sixties, in New York City on his way to a New Year's Eve Party. It was late and he'd parked his car on the corner of Madison Avenue. As he got out of the car, he heard a female voice say, "Hey you!" He could just make out the figure of an attractive woman standing in the shadows, one hand on her hip; the other beckoning him. It ran through his mind that finally a "pro" wanted him, until he realized this hot dame was his pretty sister-in-law on her way to the same party.

Still unsure if he wanted to be a minister and because his

father had urged him for years to become a lawyer, Dad entered Harvard Law School. After only one semester his low marks led him to suspect that the law was not for him. Again, the nagging desire to be a minister kept coming back. His brother, George, had decided on the ministry and was in his second year at the Virginia Theological Seminary. They still spent a lot of time with each other and at the end of that year they went on another climbing trip in Evian, France, and it was there something happened that changed Dad's life forever.

One evening after a long climb, he was in his hotel room and had what he called a "mystical experience." Filled with angst from his constantly invading thoughts about becoming a minister, he got down on his knees to pray for help. In his memoir he wrote: "For some unknown reason, I remained on my knees, waiting. At that time, I had never so much as heard of a 'mystical experience,' but I am convinced that I was granted one because, without expecting anything to happen, suddenly my 'inner self' was filled with such a sense of warmth, well-being, and joy that I wondered if my heart could endure such ecstasy." In a rush of emotion the answer became clear: He would not be a lawyer—he would follow in his brother's footsteps and become a minister. Not surprisingly, when his atheistic father discovered both of his sons were going into the ministry he said, "For years I've been teaching the basic principal that lightening can't strike the same place twice. Clearly, I was wrong!"

Dad's decision to become Reverend Trowbridge led him to the Virginia Theological Seminary in Alexandra, Virginia, and it was there that another "mystical experience" happened— he met the beautiful and talented Margaret Murdoch Laird, daughter of an Episcopal minister and granddaughter of a minister who'd been dean of a seminary. Three of her aunts had married ministers and later, her brother and several cousins became ministers (our family DNA stands for Dads, Notably Anglican). She'd already met Dad's brother, George. She and George spent much time with each other and an engagement was expected but it never happened, as one October morning when Mother was attending a tea at the Seminary, she met Cornelius. They had a long, long talk about her beloved father, laughed over childhood stories, and made a promise to see each other again, which they did almost every day. Two weeks later they met at a seminary breakfast. Sitting and talking on a bench in front of the room's fireplace, Daddy nervously poked the logs and andirons, a proposal of marriage on his mind. Working up his courage to say the words, he began to hit one of the andirons harder and harder, until at the moment he finally said, "Peggy, will you marry me?" the andiron broke in two. Two weeks later they were formally engaged and two years later, in 1924, they married.

Mr. and Mrs. Trowbridge moved to New Haven where Dad became a special student at Yale Divinity School and later received his diploma from Virginia Seminary. He was ordained at St. Paul Church in New York City and became a part-time assistant with the booming year's salary of $750. Dad was now really on his way to becoming a full-blown rector, but not before he suffered what was basically a scam.

During his years at Princeton, he'd had a friend who'd encouraged him toward the ministry and was now connected with a religious group called Buchmanism, run by Frank Buchman, who was later described as a "strange, fanatical Lutheran minister." "Buchmanism" boasted "Surrender, Sharing, Guidance, and House Parties." This was promoted as being a revival of genuine Christianity (the "house parties" being an echo of Jesus' gatherings to talk and share with his apostles). To Dad, a young man riding on new waves of enthusiasm, this seemed an important movement and he became involved with what they referred to as "The Group." However, he soon found that the "sharing" part of Buchmanism demanded open confession about sex/masturbation/homosexuality (it was later revealed that Buchman was a closeted homosexual). These revelations were deemed God's insistence that confession was the answer to everything. It soon became apparent that Buchman was taking over the role of God—a judgmental god—ignoring the parishioners from the Lower East Side who comprised the backbone of the congregation. Instead, this new religious approach was primarily directed toward those socially prominent people who were believers. Dad soon realized this "movement," later known as "Moral Rearmament" was deeply flawed.

It would come out, eventually, that Buchmanism was very harmful. For example, Glenn Close, the actress, had grown up with parents who strongly believed in Buchmanism. Close told *New York Magazine*, "It was a cult, where everyone was told to think alike, and that's devastating. I decided that I could not trust even my instincts because I didn't know what they were. Everything had been dictated to me." In the article it points out that Buchman's group had close ties to Germany, and that Buchman even attempted to meet Adolf Hitler several times. He once praised Hitler, saying, "I thank Heaven for a man like Adolf Hitler, who built a front line of defense against the anti-Christ of Communism." Needless to say, when Dad discovered the true meaning of Buchmanism, he left.

Luckily, not too much later, Dad was called to be the rector of Grace Church in Salem, Massachusetts, and in the following year he clearly experienced the effects of the Great Depression. It was during this time in 1929, that he raised money for his church's discretionary fund, a fund that helped provide minimum necessities to people in the area, helping them to weather the storm. In his memoir, Dad says, "Never was there a time when the Church was closer to her people than during this period." And never was Dad closer in contact with "all sorts and conditions of people."

While in Salem, Dad's avid belief in the good in human beings was shown by a notably documented happening. In 1934 there was a general convention of the Protestant Episcopal Church held in Atlantic City, New Jersey, its purpose to raise money. Dad, a young, unknown clergyman, attended the opening service held in an auditorium that seated twenty thousand people. The bishop of New Jersey gave a speech, pleading for funds for mission work. Dad was shocked at the low amount of money that was collected that day and encouraged the bishop to challenge the people to give more. Two days later at the missionary service, when the United Thank Offering, an organization to raise money and alleviate poverty, was to be announced, Dad was sitting in the audience holding his breath and listening to the bishop—an old tennis friend—give his second speech. Totally unaware of what he was doing, Dad walked up to the platform where the bishop was presiding and asked if he could talk to the audience. The bishop surprisingly said "Okay," and led Dad to the podium where, in stumbling sentences, he pointed out that the congregation in front of him had plenty of money to contribute a "healthy amount" and then challenged the huge gathering to come forward and make a sacrificial offering for the mission of the church. After a moment of stunned silence, people began moving forward and eventually poured more than five thousand dollars (a lot of money in those days) onto the red carpet in front of the podium. As Dad was leaving the auditorium with his mother, she asked, "Who was that young clergyman who made that wonderful appeal?" She'd been up in the gallery and her old eyes couldn't make out her son standing by the bishop, making his impassioned plea. Mother, who was visiting our Cousin Sue up in New Canaan, went to read the New York Times and was astounded to see an article with the headline, "Obscure Minister Sweeps Convention." In the article it says, "What happened is remembered as one of the most thrilling events in the Depression-depressed Church." As a result of this amazing happening, Dad was offered many jobs and soon moved to Boston where he became canon at St. Paul's Cathedral. He was now on the way to being the minister of his very own church.

During this time, Dad became involved in the Planned Parenthood League. In 1934, Massachusetts was dominated by the Catholic Church and birth control was an anathema. There was no legal selling of contraceptives and no birth control information was allowed to be doled out by physicians. Even though the law was often broken by druggists and doctors, it did little to alleviate the plight of thousands of mothers in low income brackets from being forced to give birth to unplanned babies. One Catholic doctor fought for the right of "planned parenthood" and then Margaret Sanger, whose mother had died because of diseases brought about by bearing eleven children, became the founder of the movement. Dad worked with her and on one occasion, after making a radio address directed to the Roman Catholic laity, he received hundreds of obscene phone calls. That tells it all.

Dad stayed at St. Paul's until 1940 when he was called to Chestnut Hill, Massachusetts, to be an actual rector of the Church of the Redeemer, a congregation filled with the "privileged few." By this time, he had a family boasting four children. The minister of many years before him had been fired for being a very "high churchman" (too much pomp and circumstance) so Dad was called to bring the church back down to earth. He continued his work with prisons and Planned Parenthood, but, most importantly, he was now the spiritual leader of his own church. He was the minister, and poor mother was the "minister's wife," except when we were away at our summer home. After a few years, Dad was called to Saint Peter's church in Morristown, New Jersey, the same church where Mother had permeated the sacred air with her cigarette smoke and where my siblings and I continued our fun lives as being the "minister's kids."

Dad's final church job was in 1957 when he and Mother moved to New York and lived at the famous Dakota Apartments on W. 72nd Street, the sight of John Lennon's tragic death in 1980. Dad's official job title was Director of Religious Services and Chaplin at St. Luke's Hospital. In his memoir he writes, "I was more often aware of the presence of the Living Lord in a hospital room than I had been in the chancel of a church." Most frustrating for him was dealing with patients who were incurably ill and had become "vegetables." As a result, Dad was on a televised panel discussing "the right to die." He believed that when the body can no longer function and the soul is compressed, the body should let go of the soul. There was a new movement to address the right to die and Dad worked with it until it became the Euthanasia Society, and he soon became head of the New York branch. When hearing this, I said, "Dad. I didn't know you were interested in Chinese kids!"

When I think of Dad's ministry, I think of a memorable walk I had with him when I was about fifteen. We were at Green Pastures taking our daily walk to the tennis court. We were talking about my new course in religion at school. I chose this quiet, private moment to ask about a serious subject—the virgin birth. The virgin birth would have meant a miracle and I'd always had a hard time accepting the existence of miracles. Despite my fear of posing this question, I said, "Dad, what's this thing about the 'virgin birth'?"

Dad had studied Greek, the language used to translate the Hebraic New Testament's recounting of Jesus' birth. To my astonishment, I heard my minister-father answer,

"Well, you can believe it or not, but the original Greek word meant a young woman, not a virgin."

Fascinated, I dared to ask the following: "Then what about the resurrection? Do you really think an angel rolled away the door to Jesus' tomb and then floated him up to heaven?"

Dad paused for a moment and said, "Laird, you can believe it or not. You can think of it as true or you can think of it as the best publicity stunt ever done to promote the best, kindest, most loving, wisest being ever— a man named Jesus. A man I believe ...was the son of God."

I was totally floored and burst out with, "Dad, then why are you a minister!?"

Without a pause he said "Because I believe in the fellowship of man and his creator." This conversation showed me who "Dad, the minister" was. By bringing people together in all ways, he demonstrated his belief in a fellowship of man that speaks for the reality of a God.

Dad's sense of everyday realities was demonstrated by an experience I had with him when I was in my late teens. The whole family was spending Thanksgiving with my sister, Sal, and her husband, Ernie, at their house in Wilmington, Delaware. Ernie and Sal had invited Peter, my very longtime boyfriend, who'd been Ernie's history student at the Millbrook School. Peter was the special guest. Just before lunch, Sal said loudly, "Laird, you and Peter have been dating forever—why don't you get engaged?"

Silence rang throughout the room and, at that moment, it seemed to make sense. Peter and I looked at each other and taking my hand, he led me up the stairs. We looked at each other, kissed and—yes—become engaged. Everyone was thrilled. I was numb. It all had happened so fast.

The next morning, Dad decided to go get the newspaper and I went with him. As we drove into town, I confessed that I was scared, that I didn't know whether Peter and I should get married. Dad quietly said, "Laird, marriage is a crapshoot and there's always divorce." Amazed at his practical take on such a big subject, I started to laugh and felt like I could breathe again. A few months later, I broke off the engagement. At that time in my life I was not ready to be a Mrs. It was my conversation with Dad that loosened up my mind, allowing me to face the reality of myself.

Dad died in 1972 and a few weeks later I had a mysterious experience that took the word "reality" into a different sphere. This experience harkened back to a day when I was a child walking with Dad to our tennis court in New

34

Hampshire. He was holding a can of tennis balls and I was trying to make my new sneakers look well-used by scuffing them in the dirt. Dressed in his usual white shorts and a blue T shirt, his long legs rippled with muscle; his tennis racket swung to the beat of his walk. We were talking about books; how my piano lessons were going—even talking about my problems with Mother. While we walked I could hear the click, click of what Dad called his "click (not "trick") knee". He'd acquired it from a fall while climbing in the alps. It hadn't effected his general movement or great tennis talents, but it still made a clicking sound as he walked. There always was rhythm in our walk, a rhythm to the beat of that clicking. It was our dance.

Two weeks after Dad's funeral I went to the graveyard in Princeton where he was buried. I wanted a quiet moment with him alone. After a few moments I turned to walk back to my car. Suddenly, I felt an unusual warmth throughout my body and heard that old familiar click, click of his knee. I thought to myself, "this can't be what I think it is—it must be a bird." When I stopped, the clicking stopped and there were no birds to be seen. I started walking again, and...yes...the clicking resumed. From somewhere, Dad was there with me, and I had to write this down in the rhythm of our walk:

Daddy's Knee

When walking up the dirt road
to the tennis court,
he would reach across,
take my hand and talk of
comic books, or history.
We'd joke and sing and laugh
to the click-click sound
of his "trick knee".

In his youth
he'd bruised it in a fall
and now it spoke its piece
upstairs, downstairs,
along the nighttime hall.

It was my favorite Daddy sound,
it meant that he was here,
and if he was away,
I could hear its pace
in my inner ear.

After he died,
I felt as if my breath was less
for loss of click- click beat,
until one summer day
when visiting his grave,
I heard it -(Yes!) –
as I headed for the street.

Its sound was perfect echo
of his steady walk.
and then, I felt a new,
amazing warmth
and, click, click, click,
from somewhere,
we began to talk.

Mother—two, often

3 MOTHER LOAD

When Mother wasn't sitting in our family pew in church, she was organizing things that grew, such as we and her beloved gardens. When free from her children and being "the minister's wife," she spent her time organizing the flowers and bushes in front of our houses and when at Green Pastures, pruning trees and beheading tall grasses in New Hampshire fields. When she—the champion gardener—worked on her New Hampshire gardens, they and the fields were as perfectly shaped and colorful as her

Revlon red fingernails. As she worked, her body moved like a dancer's, but her face and jaw were rigid with determination. I always suspected that when she was scything down the field grasses, she was cutting down the frustrations that lived within her. It was her garden, snuggled against the small stonewall facing the house, that gave her life as she wanted it to be; colorful, perfectly organized and obedient. Here were lilies, rosebushes, anemones and bee balm—the tall, the short, the sharp—designed to fit all moods and enclosed by constantly manicured patches of soft grass. Perfect! The only way we girls were allowed to help with the gardening was when we were commandeered to pull up dead dandelions in the hot sun for ten cents an hour. We didn't have the fun of planting a bulb and watching it grow. We were weed-whackers and nothing else.

Prize-Winning Gardener

She was a voracious, lionized gardener.
Slashed her way through jungled weed
like a murderous marine,
troweled out beds of rocky earth
with pound and punch,
force-fed them into flowering,
into perfect scheme.

She could wield a scythe
like a matador
flirting out his cape.
The grasses in the fields sighed,
grateful,
for the swiftness of her blade.

She prized her prickly thistle
and her bee balm,
praised them for their wild, unruly ways.
Her wisteria, on the wind-side, trellised easily.
Her anemones obeyed.

Roses, spotted, were her bane,
but blasted by her dust,
they grew,
as did the neighbor's potted plant,
"too near," she said, "that windowpane!"

Even the Easter lily resurrected
despite its far too northern zone.
Nothing in her plot dared die
until full-blown.

Her true green thumb was stained with nicotine.
Her harrowed soil, impervious to dew.
At night she watered us, her sprouts,
with tiny slips of bourbon;
drops of blame, undue.

She cordoned off our yard with stakes too high,
brought us up short for lack of sun,
and still we grew.
But none of us, perforce,
are gardeners.
Not a one.

Mother's handwriting, provided a clue to her personality. It was tall, straight up and down, yet at the same time, cursive, so that the letter "I" looked like the number 8. When I was at boarding school and college, anyone who searched the PO for their mail and happened to see a letter in my box, knew mother's handwriting. I'd meet a classmate on the path from the PO and she'd say, "You got a letter from your mother." I could leave her letters, no matter what they said, lying out in the open, confident that no one could decipher them. After she died, I read and re-read many of her letters, hoping to somehow find an explanation of her true self in her strange penmanship. I never could.

She was born in 1900 in the town of Arlington, Virginia. Her mother, Marion, was a beautiful woman who wore her lustrous, long hair up in a stylish roll. Her father's photographs show a handsome face with an appealing smile and deep kindness in the eyes. (The photos of Marion show that she—unlike her husband—is clearly posing for the photographer.)

Mother inherited her parents' good looks. There's a picture of her when she was about eighteen, madly paddling down a rushing river somewhere in Virginia. She is dressed in a light jacket and her curly blond shoulder-length hair is blowing out in the wind. Her curls make a halo of gold. Sadly, in the '30s, permanents became the rage and those fluffy curls were (pardon the pun) permanently gone. She became frizzed with fake curls but she still looked like Claudette Colbert— not bad at all.

She had two brothers, Bill and Ted, and the three of them were very close. Bill became a minister and Ted a surgeon. When I came down with appendicitis at college and needed surgery, I immediately went to Uncle Ted for an appendectomy. I'll never forget the moment before I was given ether to knock me out. Uncle Ted, donning his surgical mask, looked down at me. In his hands were two huge carving knives which he began to sharpen, back and forth, across one another. I gasped with laughter until the mask came down and shut me up. Mother's brothers were her close buddies, but it was her father who meant the most to her.

When she was nineteen, vacationing near Skyland

National Park in Virginia, she went on a riding picnic with friends. She was an excellent horse-woman and while riding up the hill, she suddenly stopped and inexplicably began to sob. She was slumped down over her horse's neck so her riding companions knew there was something very wrong with her or her beloved horse. They galloped up to her, but it was obvious the horse was fine and she was not. "My life is over—my life is over," she cried. She was crying so hard a young man in the group decided to take her back home and checked his watch to calculate how long it would take to get there. When they arrived, they were met with the news that her father had died of a stroke at 5:10 pm—the exact time that her friend had checked his watch! Now, with the loss of that deep connection with her father she was left alone with her mother— proper and strict. It was only when she was away from home that her keen mind and artistic talents were appreciated.

In her teens, she'd excelled at a nearby girls' school after which she got a job that introduced her to interior decorating. When not working she was dancing at beautiful parties, visiting friends and helping with church functions, but her artistry in decorating continued. After she and Dad married, her talent for color and placement grew because now she had her own house. Growing up, we called her the

Master Decorator who decorated all our family houses and all of us as well. She made many of our childhood outfits, upholstered chairs and couches, made curtains and placed all the furniture in perfect locations. She also made her own clothes, thereby doing what all minister's wives should do—save money. At one time, the managers of our Morristown parish house decided that the long green velvet curtains in the main room were too ratty and needed to be replaced. Mother, the eternal recycler of materials, took the discarded curtains and, inspired by Scarlet O'Hara in *Gone With The Wind,* made herself a glamorous evening dress. The dress had the revealing neck with the long, slender sleeve, and it fit her slim body as beautifully as Scarlet's fit hers. These days she could have had a winning career as an interior decorator, but in those days, the usual business career for women was the business of being wives and mothers.

When we were children, Anne pronounced the word Mummy as Mammy. Coming from Virginia, Mother must have known that those called Mammy were women who, at one time, had been slaves, but she loved the name. Maybe she'd had a beloved Mammy who cared for her as a child, but when I was about eight years old, one of my girlfriends heard me calling her Mammy, and said," You can't call her that. It means she's a *slave!*" She then gave me a quick lesson in the history of the South and from that time on I knew enough that Mammy was an inappropriate name for my tall, classily dressed, white mother, so I called her Mother—her title, yes— but not her nature.

Despite being the daughter of a minister, Mother prided herself on being Irene du Pont's best friend and also being related to Robert E. Lee (for this reason my sister Anne's full name was Anne Lee Trowbridge).

Daddy used to tease Mother by saying that she was going to hang herself on her family tree. He'd say that he was related to "the cooks on the Mayflower" and we'd laugh, knowing that he was saying this to tease her. One night when I was in my twenties, I went to a chichi cocktail party in Manhattan where the Christian Dior-ees were dropping names over their straight-up martinis. Trying to insult them with sarcasm, I told them, "Well, I'm related to the cooks on the Mayflower!" A handsome man standing next to me smirked at the surrounding guests and said, "Does she really think there were cooks on the Mayflower? What do you think the passengers were eating? Filet mignon? Yorkshire pudding?" It turns out we are related to Francis *Cooke* and his son, John; both passengers on the

Mayflower.

From the start of her marriage, Mother had one of the hardest jobs in the world. Being a minister's wife is a small-town version of being the First Lady. You can't move without being seen and talked about. "Oh, did you see Mrs. Trowbridge's hat on Sunday? Rather too chic, don't you think?" Mother tried to ignore parishioners' remarks, but there was one thing she couldn't ignore: that, in those days, having children was an absolute requirement for being anybody's wife.

In the '20s and '30s, when we Trowbridge children were born, the general opinion was that women were on God's earth for the sole purpose of being mothers. And having four children, especially two girls and two boys, was the perfect Woman's Home Companion recipe for life, and the quicker you did it, the better. So, soon after a miscarriage that occurred on her long honeymoon, Mother got pregnant again and gave birth to my oldest sister, Anne. It was then that she began to officially rule her roost. Anne was born in 1927, Sal in '29, Rob in '32, and I, four years later when mother was thirty-six. When I was ten years old, I found a letter, the contents of which provided a meaty subject for me and my future "shrinks" to deal with.

We'd just moved to our new rectory in Morristown and I was still getting used to our new digs. One day, bored, I climb up the creaky old stairs to the dark attic to see what my parents have stored there. The first things I see are three old wooden trunks huddled in a corner. Curious, I open one and find it's filled with cartons marked "Letters." More curious now, I open it and find a pile of letters, on top of which—amazingly—is a letter in Daddy's distinctive writing. It's addressed to Mother on the day of my birth. Breathing deeply, I carefully open the envelope and begin to read. The letter begins, "Dearie, I know you're disappointed. So am I, but we'll learn to love her anyway." I stand there looking at the words, trying to understand exactly what they mean. No matter which way I try to translate the words, it's clear to me that who I am today is not the one I was meant to be—a boy. I assume that they'd wanted another boy to have evened out our family into two girls; two boys. Not being the other son and being born four years after my brother, meant that I definitely didn't fit the Women's Home Companion specifications! It never occurred to me until then that I was a mistake; the result of an unplanned night. Decades later, just before I was to be married, I opened a memory book that mother had given me as a wedding present. Unbelievably, there on the front page was that letter. I couldn't believe it. Maybe she hadn't reread it again? Maybe she thought it funny? I pulled it out and ripped it into little pieces.

Today, I believe Mother would have been diagnosed with bipolar disorder; one of its symptoms being the need to be in control as a way to fight depression. Although she couldn't control the act of birth, she was damned good at controlling her children and her husband, as well. Because of this, Dad learned not to confront her in fear of triggering more mood swings and thereby, more trouble at home. One time when I was a teenager, Mother and I had a strong disagreement about some happening at school. She became enraged and loudly stomped upstairs. Daddy heard this fight and after she disappeared to the second floor, he came over to me and said, "Laird, you were absolutely right in what you said—but she's my wife." That told me everything. Dad was warm and comforting to his parishioners and to his children, but when Mother was around, he was as afraid as a young recruit on the firing line.

I was first confronted with mother's controlling nature when I was three years old. It's a memory deeply etched in my mind. We were at Green Pastures, our summer home in New Hampshire. It was naptime and Mother had carried me upstairs, lifted me into my crib, laid me on my back and...strapped my hands to the crib's side bars. This was done to prevent thumb-sucking.

A baby sucking her thumb had been deemed a "no no" in the early 40's. Mother had read about this method of preventing thumb-sucking in the *Ladies Home Journal,* considered a mother's bible at that time. The straps forced me to lie on my back, unable to roll side-to-side in baby style. I tried to turn over, but couldn't move. I was terrified and cried for Mother to come back, but she didn't. I was a prisoner in isolation.

As young as I was, I still remember that day. I remember it was light enough to see the picture on the wall opposite my crib. Mother had left the room and, only able to move my head, I looked to my right and, through the crib's slats, saw a tiny gray creature with pointy ears and long, thin whiskers on the sides of its mouth that twitched with excitement. For what seemed days, we stared at each other and I was fascinated by its pink eyes. Slowly, this creature—a mouse—wiggled its way between the slats and ran straight across my wide-open eyes. I remember the feel and sight of its belly—warm, white, and deliciously soft, and then, in a flash, the creature was gone.

When people hear this story they say, "Laird. You must

hate mice!" It's the opposite— I love mice. That warm little mouse gave me life while I lay strapped in a crib in an empty room, and, to this day, when I'm at our summer house in Nantucket, and the winter mouse poison has done its job, I feel a strange sadness for those sweet, soft creatures.

Thankfully, Mother discontinued this insensitive cruel practice. She'd also done this to my sister, Sal. I wasn't the only one who'd suffered tough love, it was all of us— except, of course, my brother Rob. In those days, sons were at the top of the list. But despite Mother being Captain of Conduct, I did have one experience where I physically felt and knew she was a human being, as vulnerable as the rest of us so, when I think of her, I try to focus on this memory more than my others.

Green Pastures looked directly out to Mt. Monadnock, and in the summers we had some zinger storms. Lightening would flash like a knife's blade and then thunder, sounding like a formation of tanks, would roll from the mountain across the fields and hit our house with enough force to make its old frame shudder. One day when I was small enough to be held in a parent's arms, I woke terrified from a nap as a major storm roared outside. Hearing me cry, Mother took me to her room and held me up to the window that looked out at the mountain.

Lightening was blazing. I suddenly felt her face next to my cheek and heard her whisper in my ear, "See the pretty lightening. Isn't it pretty?" It wasn't pretty to me but her whisper was a kind one, even though her arms were shaking with fear. Instinctively, I knew that she, too, was as afraid as I. She was a human being—like me. Unfortunately, these moments of kindness and connection rarely traveled from mother to child. There is one experience that best illustrates Mother's lack of connection with me. The memory of that day sticks to me as if it happened yesterday.

I am six years old and living in Chestnut Hill. One Saturday, Mammy—as I still call her—takes me to the Museum of Fine Arts in Boston. This trip is especially exciting as she rarely takes me along with her, other than when she drives me to school. When we get to the museum, she stops to read some museum pamphlets and I wander off into a side room where a small group of people are hovering over a long wooden box. I slowly move nearer to the box and, being small, the enrapt group doesn't notice me. In the box is something in the shape of a body swathed in stained white bandages. Two people carefully unwrap the bandages and, fascinated, I move a step closer. I see a bony skull and the bones of someone's chest, waist, legs, and, finally two feet, perfectly aligned side by side. My stomach churning, I run out of the room to find Mammy who's been frantically hunting for me. I tell her what I've seen and in a strict voice she says, "Laird, this wouldn't have happened if you had just stayed with me as I told you to do!" Then she adds, "But, seeing that mummy in the box must have been fascinating!" I might have used another word—like "terrifying." I needed words of comfort, but I got none.

That night, I go upstairs to my bedroom on the third story of our house to go to sleep. Down the hall is my brother's room, but he was at a friend's house for the night. I lie in bed unable to think of anything else but the engraved box and the blackened bones inside. As I lie there, I suddenly see the bones moving—at the end of my bed! The skull rises up to a sitting position and then— unbelievably—the bones begin creaking their way up until the skeleton stands straight at the foot of my bed, wisps of white cloth hanging down to the floor. I scream for Mammy to come and after what seems an eternity, I hear her running up the stairs. She opens the door, turns on the light and says, "Laird. *What* is the matter!" I point to nothing and say, "It's the mummy. It's here! It's here!" Mammy comes up to me, lays me back down in bed and staring into my eyes, quietly says, "Laird, I know it's hard, but it isn't real and you," her voice slows, "have to learn to face your fears yourself." With that, she quickly pats me on the head, turns and exits, leaving the door open a crack to the unlit hall. Many years later, as an adult, I have occasion to read some of Mother's letters and in one she mentions how her own mother taught her to "face her fears herself"—the exact words Mother spoke to me that night.

Up until we were in our late teens, Mother ruled. When at Green Pastures we had to clean the living room at 9 a.m.—no later! The newly washed dinner napkins had to be perfectly folded. During one year when we were kids, if we went two days without a bowel movement, "the bag lady" (as we called her) would come to our house carrying her big red rubber sack with the long nozzle for god awful, unnecessary enemas! Control was everything, even when it had to do with digestion. Spontaneity came second. She had learned this at her mother's sharply bent knee.

We called Mother's mother, Granny Laird. As many of her family members died during her early years, her growing up was sad, but she put her talents to good use and became a founder and hard-worker for an organization that promoted education for needy children. To us, she was hardly your idea of a typical old granny. Yes, her hair was graying but it was long and full, swept up and worn as a crown on her head. She was tall and had high cheekbones, like Mother. She was so gorgeous, in fact, that on one occasion she was chosen, not by the best man in the world, but by the worst.

This happening occurred in the early '30s before World War II. Granny Laird, recently widowed, went to Germany with her son, Ted, who wanted to be a doctor. As the result of the Great Depression, American medical schools were very expensive and therefore many aspiring doctors went abroad to study. Ted went to a university near Berlin and Granny went with him. staying in Berlin just long enough to help him get settled.

One evening she went to the opera with a woman she'd met. They were seated a short way back from the front row which was occupied by men in uniform. As usual, Granny Laird was elegantly dressed and striking in a long velvet skirt and silk blouse. During the intermission, a young soldier walked up the aisle and stopped at her row. He stared at her and then, looking back to the front, he shook his head at someone and waved his hand side-to-side, signaling, "No." That "someone" was dressed in a very official Army uniform. That someone was Hitler. In Granny's recount of that night, she figured out that the shake of the head showed that upon staring at her, Hitler's adjutant had realized she was too old for Hitler's likes.

Being an excellent pianist, music was one of Granny's great loves. Her hands were slim and smooth and her fingers long on the keys. When she came to visit us and a scary thunderstorm raged outside, she'd play Chopin's "Raindrop Serenade" to distract us, inviting us to think of soft rain instead of the storm, and it helped. One night, when she and I were in the house alone, the non-musical side of her character, however, clearly showed itself.

My parents were out to dinner and my siblings away at school. Granny was left with the chore of feeding me supper. She'd made tapioca pudding for dessert. I have always detested the taste and consistency of tapioca pudding, with those little bumpy eyes you had to swallow. But, that night, Granny commanded me to clean my bowl because of "all the starving children in Armenia." She demanded I sit at the table until I finished the white gooey stuff in the bowl. I sat there alone for an hour while Granny came in and out, saying, Tapioca, Laird! Tapioca!" I was determined. I won the pudding standoff. Granny had to let me up as she finally realized I would probably last out the night—as I would have.

There was one glorious Thanksgiving lunch back when we lived in Chestnut Hill. Granny had come to visit and, for dessert, Mother served macaroons with ice cream and berries. Granny took a bite of her macaroon and her incessant talking came to a sudden stop. We watched her there with her mouth shut in a tight line, and her jaws straining up and down, her teeth stuck on the macaroon. Mother said, "Just open your teeth slowly, Mother." Granny tried this, but it didn't work. Then, to our amazement, she put her thumb into her mouth and, suddenly, out popped the macaroon and Granny's false front teeth. There was our regal grandmother, her mouth wide open with two long Dracula fangs hanging down. It was a terrible moment for her and, sensing this, we did not laugh but put our heads down while Granny sneaked out— choppers and macaroon in hand.

Another, far more telling, story about our southern Granny took place in Morristown when Daddy had arranged a dinner for certain visiting ministers. They were in town helping Dad to encourage Episcopal churches in the area to be more of what was known as "low church" with simpler rituals than of a "high church." Granny was, again, visiting. Dad, held up at a meeting, wasn't there to greet the visitors, so she took over as hostess. After some sherry in the living room, she led the ministers to the dining room and their designated seats. After a few moments, the doorbell rang and in came the final guest, who happened to be an African American minister.

As the story goes, Granny led him into the living room, gave him a glass of sherry and then had our maid quickly set up a card table and cover it with a table cloth and silverware...in the living room. Granny explained to him that she was so sorry, but they hadn't expected him. This was a blatant lie. There was an empty place setting for him at the dining table. Granny was from the South and this is how she'd been brought up. Apparently, though, the African American minister made no objection and sat quietly where he'd been placed. At this point Daddy arrived and immediately saw what Granny had done. Stunned by her action, he quietly commanded her to move the banished minister to the main table. Daddy whispered apologies in the minister's ear and the minister said, "Don't worry, Reverend Trowbridge. It happens all the time." Needless to say, Daddy and Granny were not close. Maybe that is why he referred to her as "Madam."

Mother's lack of warmth was partially due to her strict bringing up, but most of it, I know now, was due to depression. Little was known about depression in the '30s. What Mother suffered from was known, then, as "mood disorder" for which she was given medicine, including Phenobarbital for her lungs. None of these prescriptions worked. Today, she would have been diagnosed as having a form of bipolar disorder, and I'm sure today's drugs would have helped, but back then little was available.

Despite her lack of warmth with her children, Mother could show great sympathy for others. I remember one such occasion when we were living in Chestnut Hill and were lucky enough to have a wonderful maid named, Priscilla, who had a boyfriend named Bill who was a sergeant in the Army. We'd met him twice when he was stationed nearby and had come to visit Priscilla. He'd played with us and treated us like family. In his sergeant's uniform he'd become a hero to us all. I'll never forget the day that Priscilla was notified that her Bill had been killed while on a navy warship. I was in the kitchen when the phone rang to tell Priscilla of Bill's death. Mother answered the call and, tears in her eyes, came into the kitchen to hug Priscilla and tell her the news. Priscilla stared at Mother in shock and then bent over a kitchen chair and sobbed uncontrollably. Mother rubbed her back to quiet her down and then took her home. I remember Mother's unusually warm, loving behavior that day. Sadly, that kind of warmth was seldom seen.

My first experience of Mother's depression came when I was about four years old. Daddy had gone upstairs to find Mother and she was gone. She'd been in the house a short time before and because he knew of her mood swings, and maybe because she'd done this before, he decided he'd take the car and try to find her. Because I was too young to be left alone, he bundled me up and put me in the car beside him. We drove around for a long time and, finally, ended up at the church—right next door to our house. Dad opened the side door of the church and there was Mother, sitting in a pew, her head down, weeping. I was given no explanation for her disappearance, just quickly driven home and put to bed. I knew something was very wrong because, young as I was, I had heard many kinds of crying coming from Mother, whimpering crying and angry sobbing. But I'd never witnessed this kind of crying. It was without noise— just a bent head, tears running down her cheeks. From then on, we all learned to simply wait it out. She'd cry at strange times. Daddy might be reading aloud in the living room at

Green Pastures and there would be Mother painting her
nails, tears silently spilling onto her hands. You never knew
when it would happen or why. It might happen in church; it
might happen at dinnertime.

Early Dinner

All that summer
we ate at twilight,
piled our sibling din
on shifting plates of silence
in the tableland
between the two of them.

Butter-knives scraped china to the bone.
Chair backs rocked convenient creaks.
Sneakers drummed tattoos on table legs.
Jokes, like hand-grenades,
were lobbed
to clear the silence in the room.

"Pass the chicken."
"Pass the gravy."
Pass the laughter,
toss it off for safety
like salt behind the back,
like never stepping on a crack,
like upheld cross.

Above all. Chat.
About the weather,
the new girl down the road.
Should we ask her over?
Sing the latest school song.
Anything. Whatever.
Make some sound

to cover
for our eyes
flitting to table's ends,
He, with plastic smile—
She, her head down, teary,
yet, again.
We, wondering, beneath our noise,
if her tears—
his movie smile—
would, somehow,
mend.

Mother's crying made me feel as if Mr. Death lived in our house. He certainly lived in the church next door where we heard that scary story of the man who suffered a torturous death on a cross. He definitely lay under stones in the graveyard right by our house and often he would roll up to the church lying in a box in the back of long black car. Sometimes he even was dressed in a tweed skirt and cardigan sweater—like Mother's.

When Mother slipped into her cold moods of depression—she drank. Then, she became angry and threatened to leave—forever. If confronted, especially by high-tempered, Anne, she would explode with rage, stomp into her room, slam the door behind her and shout, "I give up! I wish I were dead! I might as well kill myself!" Being the youngest, I would be sleeping but her shouts would wake me and I would hear what she said. My heart would race as I imagined her downing a whole bottle of sleeping pills. Some nights I would creep into her room, tiptoe to her bed, and lean down to see if she was still breathing. (Because of his locomotive snoring, Daddy slept in a different room and, being a heavy sleeper, didn't hear.

Despite the deeply dark side of Mother, she, thank God, had a humorous side as well—Dad wouldn't have married her if she hadn't—but with her children the spontaneous back and forth exchanges of jokes, or the fun of friendly teasing, was rarely shared. With us, Mother's humor was an event that we longed to attend more often. It was a rare event but when it came—it was unforgettable.

During our first week living in Morristown, a week before Christmas, we'd not been in our rectory home long enough to be totally familiar with its large spaces. There were mysterious little halls that ran from the main areas of the house in and out of little rooms on the three floors of this huge rectory. Next week we might know our way around, but this week we still needed a map of this three-storied stone manse, so unlike our previous small clapboard rectory in Chestnut Hill.

Mother needed no map. She knew every nook and cranny and could have walked it at night wearing a blindfold. Even more amazing was that she, the interior decorator, had beautifully arranged everything in the house and was now in the process of decorating our high-ceilinged library for the holidays. She'd bought a Christmas tree so tall it could have come from Muir Woods. After much pushing and lifting, it now stood at the back of the room. If you came in the front door and took your first left, you were in the library. If you took your second left you were faced with one of those little halls, at the end of which was a door to a bathroom.

Mother had inherited ancient Christmas decorations from Dutch ancestors who lived in the mid 1800's. There were boxes filled with large bulbs, faded, but still twinkling with smoky coatings of blue, gold, and silver, and there were old hanging crystals in gold frames, ornaments that could never be replaced and which were never handled by anyone but her. Dad's job was to top the tree with our usual star and we kids were permitted to help with the tinsel ropes, the icicles, and the cheap, new ornaments. The tree, itself, was secured to the back wall with thin wires, and there was only just enough space for our beloved golden star at the top.

One evening, as we were decorating the tree, Dad wandered around looking for the bathroom. He finally found it at the end of the little back hall and proceeded to take a leak. We, busily trimming the tree, heard him flush the toilet and then, to our horror, he opened the bathroom's inside door—the one that opened into the library. Frozen, we watched as the door hit the tree. We heard the wires snap and then, trying to reach the tree, Dad stumbled head first into its branches. The mammoth tree tilted forward, forward, forward. Mother, smoking and dressed in her red Christmas sweater, was standing in the main hallway looking at this slow motion movie. She didn't move an inch. She didn't run with arms stretched toward the tree shouting, "Corny! Don't let it fall!" something we all expected. Instead, she stood, tall and very quiet. Then, slowly raising her arms in a give-up sign to heaven, she looked up, smiled and quietly said, "Timmmmmmmmber." There was nothing left to do but roar with laughter—and we all did.

Another Mother-laugh happened at a Sunday lunch, again in Morristown. Every Sunday, Mother served a half a

64

grapefruit on a glass plate, a silver fruit fork lying correctly by its side before the main course of roast chicken or baked ham. On this day, Rob, seated next to her, was describing a scene in a movie where James Cagney squishes a grapefruit into someone's face. Rob said, "How did he do it without laughing?" and, as if on cue, Mother, the Virginia Lady, picked up her grapefruit, turned to Rob, squished it in his face and with a straight face said, "Like this?" We were astounded, but if Mother could do this—couldn't we? Immediately, we all grabbed our grapefruits and squished them in the faces of those to our right. I got to do Mother's and—yes, there is a God—she laughed as the seeds and fruit flesh spread across her face.

Rob was the cause of another mother-episode. In my young years, Rob rarely had anything to do with me except harmonizing with me in our family songfests. I was the small brat who didn't play boy-sports and ran around with idiot young girls. The only time he deigned to treat me as an equal was when we played Batman and Robin. I, of course, was Robin—the lesser character in both height and importance. We would pin towels on our shoulders and run through the house, always looking back to see if our "capes" were flying. One Sunday afternoon, we were racing around upstairs, looking backwards, and Rob tripped on the top stair and then rolled head over heels down the stairs, ending up with his head deep into the base of our antique grandfather clock. Mother was giving one of her hated parish teas. Little old ladies were wandering around with tiny cups of tea in their white-gloved hands. Suddenly, they saw this masked, tall boy hurtle down the stairs and crash into the beautiful clock a few feet away from them. With their gloves covering their mouths, the guests gasped with ladylike horror. As Rob began to extract his head from the clock—thankfully very much alive—Mother turned to the ladies, pointed to Rob and casually said "I'd like you to meet my son, Rob." Luckily Rob survived with only a large bump, but the grandfather clock, which now lives in our house, has a permanent diagonal crack at its bottom. Every time I pass it I mentally say hello to him.

I have mentioned Mother's extraordinary telepathic ability, first documented by her collapsing at the exact time of her father's death. Another inexplicable example of this gift occurred years later when she lost the small, beautiful diamond watch Daddy had given her as an engagement present. This happened during the summer and, despite our constant on-going searches throughout the house and outside, when January came, we hadn't found it. One night we had a major Boston snowstorm and during the night the driveway was plowed, leaving high banks of snow along its sides. Early in the morning Mother woke up, walked directly out to a snow bank on the driveway, stopped, and there, face up in the snow, was her watch. She told us she'd seen the watch in a dream. Because of the nighttime plowing it was impossible that she could have seen the watch the day before or during the night. When these events happened, Daddy would say "Oh, there she goes again," brushing off the reality of these happenings, just as he often brushed off the reality of her.

I've always been curious about Mother and Dad's marriage and whether it was good or bad. I know from letters that they were very much in love when they married. The very first letter Dad wrote to her starts out, "I'm in love and you're it!" There are early photos of them hugging and winking at the camera. There is one of mother leaping across our lawn at Green Pastures, her arms and smiling face lifted to the sky, but these photos were taken early on in their married lives— before they had children. I know from walking in on them one night that they had a sex life, but I've always thought that Dad may not have been the easiest husband to live with. Because of his casual ways and being the center-stage minister, Mother often had to force herself into the center of their social life. And no doubt she had a problem with being expected to be Mrs. Minister. I know that they were happiest when in crowds of friends—there are pictures of them laughing it up at parties—but when alone, they were too often at odds. This may have led to the following mystery.

From early on, excessive cigarettes contributed to Mother's congestive kinds of colds—aka—"The Bug," resulting in her taking to bed for long periods of time. She would lie there bundled up, coughing up phlegm, her voice sounding like a growling dog. We'd bring meal trays and clean her room until, finally, she was able to come downstairs. But then "The Bug" would come again. One winter it was so bad that her doctor advised her that being in a warm, dry climate would make all the difference and knowing of a ranch near Tucson, Mother packed up and left for what we were told would be a two-week trip. Mother loved riding so she was ecstatic to be getting away from a Boston winter and being back on a horse. It wasn't two weeks, but six weeks later, that she came home. Apparently, it had taken her that long to get over her on-going respiratory problems ... apparently.

The day she came home and drove up the driveway, we all greeted her with welcome-home signs. She was tanned and smiling, but she immediately went to bed to rest up from her trip. Within a couple of days, a small box arrived, addressed to her with the return address of a Mr. Bob Russell, the owner of the ranch. In the box was a small, china figurine of an elephant in an envelope, on top of which was written, "An elephant never forgets." We all— especially Daddy—wanted to know what the note referred to and Mother quickly explained that Bob Russell had been very kind in his efforts to successfully reintroduce her to the joys of riding. But when these little boxes kept coming and coming, we became very curious. Daddy would take them from the postman and yell upstairs to Mother, "It's Old Bob Russell again!" "Old Bob Russell" became a household joke until, twelve boxes later, the elephant deliveries finally stopped. Each elephant was different. Today, they line one of my bookshelves, all of them made of different material—glass, straw, ivory, metal, and wood—and to this day I wonder about the meaning of those elephants. Yes, Dad and Mother walked together, talked together, laughed together but to very different tempos.

I always try to think of the humorous times with Mother but, despite my efforts, there are childhood dreams and letters that tell the truth of how much she scared me. In one dream Mother and I are standing by an old stone watering well in the town square of an ancient town in some foreign country. I am bent over and looking down at the water. Suddenly, I feel her hand on the back of my head, slowly pushing me down toward the water. She leans down to my ear and softly says, "It won't take a minute, Laird." She is going to drown me, a metaphor for the reality of our relationship. The most telling dream of Mother was born from an experience I had when I was young and helping Dad get our Green Pastures tennis court ready for our summer games. Dad's job was to lay out the tapes that shaped the court. My job was to sweep them clean. One day, while doing my job, I saw a round black, mammoth object coming from the grass. It was wiggling back and forth as it crawled toward the center of the net. I was terrified and screamed as I pointed to the Thing on the court. Dad grabbed my broom, ran to the Thing and whacked it. Immediately, a million tiny black dots swarmed over the court, baby spiders who'd been clinging to the back of their large spider mother. When all the spiders were swept away, Daddy explained to me that mother spiders carry their young on their backs, especially if they are coming out of large fields and that my sweeping probably had caused the mother spider to appear and spill her babies.

Years later, in my dream, I hear a rattling noise in my closet and, thinking a mouse must be running through my shoes, I take a broom and open the door to chase the mouse away. Suddenly, a wide dark circle of something on the floor wiggles its way toward me. I look closer and, to my horror, the circle is a huge, black spider. I take a broom and hit it and off its back come a thousand tiny, spider-like figures of—Mother. These two dreams clearly illustrate my childhood fright of her.

My fright echoed itself in letters I wrote her, which she kept in a box, with the word "Laird!!!" on top. One clearly shows the way I had to show myself to Mother. On the one hand, I had to agree with her ratings of me; on the other, I had to show her that I loved her. This letter, written when I was fifteen years old ends with "Please, say we turn over a new leaf. I'll try like hell and when I try, will you try, too? Please, try to understand your adolescent, unloving, selfish, disobedient, rude, contradicting, spoiled, hurting, Queen of Sheba, 'talented' daughter." And then, in very small letters it reads, "I really do love you, you know!" Yes. She thought I was "talented," but she also thought I was all the other adjectives and, despite her use of these, I knew I had to say, "I love you"—for safety's sake.

I once said to a therapist, "How can I complain about my mother? After all, I wasn't physically abused." She explained to me that slow, continuous emotional abuse may be harder to recover from than the immediacy of physical abuse. She told me to imagine two people sitting in chairs on a stage. One is wrapped in thick ropes of physical abuse; the other is wrapped in a coat of fine threads of constant emotional pain. The person strapped by thick rope is able to manipulate the rope into allowing a space from which to escape. With strong pulling, the rope will fall away. The other must find the end of the miniscule thread and slowly unwind it to be free. As the strings are so thin as to be almost invisible, the unwrapping will take a long, long time. On-going emotional abuse is like being entwined by the fine threads of fear, forcing one to unwrap for sometimes years, before becoming free. It has taken me years to unwrap those threads to the point where they can be squashed into a ball and thrown away. Whenever those scary memories come, I toss out that ball of fear and say, "Laird, she was emotionally sick."

Mother's heart began to fail and a year or so after Dad's death she died of an over-dose of Adrenalin which had been prescribed for her fibrillating heart. Up until her death she was still drinking and smoking, vices that she had learned from Dad. When Sally called to tell me Mother had died, I sighed an audible sigh and said, "It's terrible, but I'm relieved." Sally said she was, too. It wasn't just that we were relieved that she was free from pain, it was that we were relieved that we were free from dealing with her troubled nature.

When I think of her now, I lift my head to the skies and say, "Where ever you are, Mother, I hope you're sitting with a baby on your lap, making that baby smile." Then, I think about that grapefruit on her face, the laughter in her eyes—and I smile.

4 TONY, NEXT DOOR

Even though Mother's controlling nature played the lead role in my early life, there was a time when I found protection right next door. Dad had become Rector of the Church of the Redeemer in Chestnut Hill, on the outskirts of Boston. I was four years old. Up to then, our "on-the-job mother" had been an Irish maid who took care of me and my siblings. Now, with Dad's new job starting, we'd become "PK's"—preacher's kids—and as WWII was revving up, money was low, and for the first time, Mother had to act the mother.

She did not have a smile on her face when we moved to Chestnut Hill. Life was going to be very different. She would be watched and minister-wife smiles would be required at all times. She would have to decorate our small rectory and make it a proper site for parish teas and meetings and she would have to—oh God—care for me. At this time, my two older sisters were away at school; my brother went to a local boys' school and hardly paid any attention to me, and Dad was consumed with work. However, soon after we moved, luck was with me and I discovered a new friend my age right next door and, despite the fact that he was a boy, maybe we could be friends? We not only could—we did.

His name was Tony Winsor and after a very short time he became not only my friend, but my savior—not the one in the Bible or up in the heavens, but the one just beyond the narrow line of trees and the stone wall that separated our homes. I knew him from age four until ten and in those years he became my brother.

Tony was a thin boy with a tiny protruding stomach and the biggest stick-out ears I'd ever seen. He had dark hair, darkish skin and an impish smile that, when laughing, spread from one big ear to the other. He usually wore striped t-shirts that accentuated his apple stomach, but I didn't care—he accepted me, not as a mere girl, but as a pal to play with. The two of us went to the same school and we walked there together every day. During holidays my siblings came home and we had fun, but it was Tony and his family that came first in my life.

When Tony and I would come home from school, we'd often see his father raking leaves or pruning bushes; he was part of the landscape. He was a tall, hefty man with graying hair and I never saw him in anything but rumpled gray flannel trousers, scuffed brown shoes with rubber soles, a beige V-necked cardigan over a plaid shirt and on his head, a brown fedora. Although cigarettes were fashionable during the forties, he smoked nothing but an old wooden pipe and smoked it constantly. When inside, he would retire behind his newspaper, smoke encircling his head like Santa Claus and let the verbosity of his wife, son, and daughter storm around him while he remained calm in the eye of their hurricane. He'd just sit there, as quietly as if he were in a public library. When I came into a room where he was reading, he would wink at me. He exuded warmth. My favorite times with him were during the fall when Tony and our friend, Johnny McDuffy, roasted baked potatoes in the huge piles of leaves Mr. Winsor had raked up. With the war always on our minds, Tony and Johnny would jump in and out of the piles of leaves pretending they were parachuting to land; they'd shoot imaginary guns at each other or pelt each other with grenades of balled up leaves. Rarely would they allow me to join in the war games. I wasn't the WAC, I was simply the girl, so I would stand safely by Mr. Winsor and wait for the boys to get tired and the potatoes to be done.

Mrs. Winsor was a thin, plain woman who was always busy. She baked cookies, folded laundry, washed the kitchen floor, vacuumed, and did all the housekeeping chores, but she always had time to talk with me about school or piano lessons. Even my young mind knew she had a "cat's cradle" connection to everyone around her. Carla, Tony's tall, glamorous sister, would streak through the house in a teenage mood and, instinctively, I knew Mrs. Winsor understood exactly what the problem was and that Mr. Winsor didn't. He let that be his wife's department.

Mother, not wanting to be bothered, would encourage me to go "visit the Winsors." During one visit, Mrs. Winsor asked me what scared me the most and I told her about my experience with the mummy. She stressed the fact that it was only a dream and that if I let her take me to the same museum she would stay with me and we'd see some wonderful things ... not just mummies. I agreed to go and was able to look at the mummies and soon fascination overtook fright and I actually became seduced by the mystery of buried ancient objects. As a result, Daddy told me about the ancient Egyptians. I became so fascinated with King Tut and archeology, that every fall I would bury one of my dolls in our backyard and then dig it up in the spring. Mother thought this was crazy, but Mrs. Winsor would pretend fascination when I showed her the dirt covered, bug-eaten, ancient being I'd excavated.

Having become great friends, Tony and I couldn't stop talking so we rigged up a telephone line between our houses, consisting of a very long string with paper cups at the ends. Every night we'd chat, bedroom to bedroom, across the bushes and plot of grass that separated our homes until sleep silenced us. Most of the time I'd be at his house happily feeling a member of the Windsor family. Mrs. Windsor sometimes had me spend the night and put Tony and me in the same room where we talked the night away in two old twin beds. After all, I was his sister, wasn't I? It didn't matter that we were boy and girl.

The first time I realize that Tony's actually a boy is on a rainy day when we're playing the piano in his living room. He's wearing the usual striped t-shirt that fits snuggly over his little belly just above his shorts. This day, he says something that breaks us up and, gasping with laughter, he starts to pee on the Winsor's lovely oriental rug. Suddenly, he looks down at the growing puddle of pee, takes his penis out of his pants, shakes it, and says, "Bad boy!" It was at that moment that I first see what that thing really looks like.

The war became a constant third party to Tony's and my relationship. With the help of his father, Tony had fashioned two pieces of wood into the shape of rifles and every morning before school he and I would meet outside and go through Army drill exercises—twirling the rifles, thumping them on the ground, kneeling and pointing them at imaginary enemies—just like we'd seen on the movie news. This was how we started the day and if I came late for our meeting, Tony, smiling, would chastise me in Sergeant-like fashion. Then, we'd be off to school. We did this every school day and on the weekends when we were allowed to roast potatoes in the ever-present brush fire, we'd slather the potatoes with butter and salute each other in recognition of a good Army mess-hall meal. One of our teachers was as strict as a drill sergeant to the point of meanness, thus becoming our own "enemy." Could we attack her with our guns or maybe set off a bomb under her desk? When talking about her in public we called her Glinda— the name of the wicked witch in The Wizard of Oz— so as not to be punished for our terrorist talk.

Tony, the male soldier and thereby the one in command, decided that he, himself, had to fight the enemy and one day I was designated to be "it!" He deemed me "The German," making me stand on a rock without moving. He whispered, "If you move, I'll shoot you!" Fortunately, Mrs. Windsor came out to hang up the laundry and I was rescued. On another day I was the Japanese soldier and he tied me up in the family's weathered garage; made me sit with my bare ankles tied in a rope and spread talcum powder around my feet. He told me the powder was quicklime from his father's garden. He said to me, "If you take off your sneakers and try to escape, your feet will burn off." I sat there rigid for what seemed a day until I was finally rescued by Mr. Windsor who came to the garage for a tool of some sort. Tony's parents sent him to his room for a whole day and Tony apologized to me with tears in his eyes. I was never made the enemy again.

One of my most embarrassing childhood memories is about the time Tony and I put on a play for our parents and siblings. The war was still being fought and having sneaked into the local movie theater to see a war movie, we were deeply into death from battle and, as in typical war movies, there is the question: When man leaves woman to go to war, will he return? Does she fall in love with someone else while her husband is away? Will he fall in love with a WAC, or an Army nurse? Even for us, the war was a day-to-day drama, so why not dramatize it? And, on a sunny Sunday afternoon, we did.

It being summer, Sal, Anne and Rob were home awaiting the time when we'd leave for Green Pastures. Tony and I had decided that we'd do the play on the small grassy level that bordered the back of his house. The grass sloped down to the lawn where Mr. Winsor had set up folding chairs for the audience. The only props I remember from this epic drama were the dish towel I carried, the apron around my waist (pointing out that I'm a "wife") and the Army-like jacket that Tony, the soldier, wore. We'd put out two chairs, a lamp and two tables, one holding a dish rack full of dishes, the other, a vase of flowers. An American flag was hanging over the back door. The rest of the stage was left to the audience's imagination.

The first act consisted of me—the happy wife—drying the dishes. Then, Tony comes home from work and tells me he has been called to war. I start weeping into my dishtowel. I am devastated and grasp him in my arms. We bend in a phony kiss and Tony exits around the side of the house. In the second act I vacuum the house and read a letter from my soldier-boy to the audience. This indicates the passing of time. Then comes the third act. Tony returns home, limping on a cane, knocks on our imaginary door and enters, bent over, one leg bandaged from ankle to thigh. Needless to say, I look at him, horrified; put my dishtowel up to my eyes and screaming "Oh, no!," I rush to take him in my arms and yes— kiss him right next to his mouth.

We finished this agonizing scene with the two of us walking out the door smiling at each other, my hand covering his (the one grasping the cane) showing that, despite war's damage, we will be together—forever—through our changed life.

It was a heart-wrenching, triumphal moment worthy of an appropriately named, Tony Award. Then came the glorious sound of applause. We rushed back to take our bows. Looking down at the audience I saw Anne, her hand covering her widely grinning mouth, her body shaking with laughter. I didn't care. I got to kiss Tony—almost on the mouth.

My Tony Award!

In 1946, when I was ten, we moved to Morristown and I had to say goodbye to Tony and his family. It was one of the saddest goodbyes of my life. Tony and I kept up for a short time with funny cards and an occasional call with his mother in the background, but those ties slowly dwindled.

Sometime in my late twenties I got an unexpected call from Tony's mother, telling me that he was engaged to a nice girl and was getting married the following month. I somehow felt abandoned and sad until she said, "Laird, when Tony told me he was engaged, I felt I had to tell him it was time to remove the Captain Midnight ring you'd given him— the one he keeps on his keychain." I remember I teared up but in my heart I felt happy and again, next door to my brother, Tony. What Mrs. Winsor had told me was like receiving a love letter that had been lost in the mail for years. He and I were no longer next door to each other, but we were in each other's minds. Time hadn't wiped us out, but, instead, had brought us together.

A few years ago my niece, Peggy, wanted to have her wedding take place where Sally, her mother, had been married— Dad's old church in Chestnut Hill. I hadn't seen the place since I was ten. The wedding was lovely and I kept hearing Dad's distinct voice echoing from the pulpit. After the service, I went up to the minister and asked him if the Winsor family were anywhere around. I briefly told him about my relationship with Tony and his family and how much they'd meant to me. He smiled, pointed to the old house next to our old home and said, "Tony's right there!" I couldn't believe it. My husband, Reid, and I went over and knocked on the door.

A pretty woman opened the door and I quickly told her who I was and she said, "Oh yes. I remember your name!" She asked us to come in and told us that Tony was in the living room—the room where he'd peed. Then, she said, "I want to warn you. Tony has early Alzheimer's so he may not remember you well." Having heard voices in the front hall, Tony came out to see who was there. His wife turned toward me and said, "This is your old friend, Laird Trowbridge and her husband." Tony bent his head forward and stared at me. I figured that he had no idea who I was but, suddenly, he smiled, put his arms out and said, "Laird!" We hugged and I knew from the smile and the hug that he remembered—perhaps not everything—but at least the fact that we'd been very good friends. A few years ago Tony died of Alzheimer's disease. I was grateful for that hug.

Despite having to leave Tony when we moved to Morristown, I still had one familiar friend next door—not a live one in a striped t-shirt but a well-known neighbor—the church. For all of us Trowbridge kids, the church was not just a Sunday building, but a Sunday pal.

5 "HI, CHURCH!"

No matter where we lived, we had a neighbor next door—
our church. It was there when we woke up, when we came
home from school, and when we went to bed. It was cared
for in the summers by Dad's assistant who practiced his
soon-to-be ministerial preaching. It was our down-to-earth
friend who was by our side every day.

None of Dad's churches were deemed "High Church".
If Dad had been a 'High Church" minister, we would have
been praying at night on our knees— "forever and ever,
Amen." No, each of his churches was a friendly stone
neighbor and, as a kid, I'd wake up in the morning,
knowing that my friend was there.

While church was a part of the family; a place filled with Dad's captivating sermons, beautiful organ music, and sometimes mischievous fun, one Christmas Eve, it was the home of near disaster.

Every year, two days before Christmas, Mother would turn us into Santa's elves and give us jobs decorating the church for the Christmas Eve service. She would donate vases and bowls filled with fruit to be carried down the aisle by those playing the townspeople who'd come to worship the newborn babe. She'd make Mary's light blue cowl and all other costumes. Dad would be up at the podium, reading the biblical account of Jesus' birth and behind him, standing on risers in the apse, four angels would be standing with Angel Gabriel at the very top. The girl playing Gabriel was dressed in a white robe with beautiful wings spread wide to the world. The lights would shine down on the angels, and it was a heavenly sight to see. To get to be the Angel Gabriel, a girl was required to be a little angel praying at the foot of baby Jesus' crèche for many years of Christmas pageants. After that, if she was lucky, she was promoted to be Angel Gabriel on top of the risers.

I've got a crèche on you

On this particular Christmas Eve, the service was held in the "holy smoke" church where Mother had become famous. I had been honored with the role of cherub at one end of the crèche; my sister Sal had been promoted to Angel Gabriel. She and her fellow angels were standing there in the dark and everyone knew that when Daddy's sermon ended, Mrs. King, the church vocalist, would burst into song. Mrs. King's voice was famous. It was as loud as a trumpet. Every Christmas, she would sing the oratorio from Handel's "Messiah" beginning "Fear not! For behold... I bring you good tidings of great joy." It was at this moment that the spotlights would hit the angels.

This night, after Daddy had finished the Bible's account of Jesus' birth, Mrs. King began her aria and the lights suddenly hit the angels. Up and out of Mrs. King's canyon size mouth came, "FEAR NOT!"—so loud that members of the congregation shook in their seats. Then, over and above Mrs. King's voice, came a loud crack. To our horror, Sally, shocked by Mrs. King's blast of sound, jerked backwards and broke one of the riser's slats. We could see her wobbling back and forth, her arms flailing to maintain her balance. Her huge white feathery wings flapped as she teetered six feet above the apse's tiled floor. The four angels below were reaching up, trying to save Gabriel from a fall from grace.

I remember looking up from my place at the crèche wondering if my beloved sister was falling to her death? Would she go to Heaven? Daddy's hands were pressed against his mouth in terror for what, surely, would end in disaster. Miraculously, Angel Gabriel was an athlete, and, by waving her hands and bending her knees, she was able to keep herself balanced on the remaining slat. Then, she slowly stood and raised her arms to heaven. The congregation slumped back in their pews and sighs of relief were heard throughout the church. Of course! How could we ever, even for a moment, have feared that the Angel

Gabriel could crash to earth and not rise again? But then, to our horror, we heard another crack. The other slat had broken and Gabriel plummeted to the floor. But, miraculously—that athletic angel rolled like a football player and sat up, unscathed. The other four angels came down from the risers to see if she was all right. After a second, Gabriel raised one hand, pointed to heaven and said, "Thanks, God!" The congregation burst into thankful laughter. Then, Mrs. King began to sing, softly this time. Her hands were clasped and raised in honor of Angel Gabriel's resurrection.

There were many less dramatic happenings, but still ones that brought on those "church giggles." One regular parishioner, Mrs. Abeel, a woman who we knew only by sight, came every Sunday service with her daughter, Daphne, but they always came late. Mrs. Abeel was tall and always wore bright, knitted dresses or jackets which she'd designed herself. Daphne was rather short and always dressed conservatively. Their pew was in the side chapel of the church, right in front of our good friends, the Savages, whose son, Arthur, was Anne's age and had a very dry wit and a beautifully deep voice.

One Sunday, Daphne and her mother arrived late as always. Mrs. Abeel was wearing one of her usual Sunday knits. It boasted a brown and orange triangular pattern with the tips of the triangles meeting each other at her waist, making it impossible for anyone looking at her not to think of a backgammon board. When she sat down, the nearby parishioners looked at each other and smiled their usual smiles. Suddenly Arthur's low, but audible voice said, "Your move!" and, getting the joke, everyone in the chapel tried to stifle laughs. Arthur never did this again, but Mrs. Abeel, in her backgammon dresses, became a treasured Sunday sight. Years later when we noticed Mrs. Abeel was no longer appearing in church, we heard that she'd died quite suddenly. We all were very sad. We missed our beloved Backgammon Lady.

"Hi, church" happenings often spilled over into our house, usually at Sunday lunches. Daddy had a penchant for asking those who were alone and needy to our family-style Sunday lunches where we dined on over-cooked roast beef, potatoes, and boiled vegetables, thankfully blessed with pie and ice cream for dessert. These "charity lunches" mostly took place in our Morristown rectory.

One Sunday, Daddy invited Mrs. Osborn, a widow who lived alone in a Victorian house down the road. She was an old lady, thin and hunched over, and she always wore a small, dark brimmed hat pulled down to her eyebrows. She never took it off. She had come to lunch before and, as usual, was correctly seated to Daddy's right, and we four kids were spread around the long table that glittered with silver cutlery and crystal glassware. Mother was at table's head, dressed in her tweed, rose-colored Sunday suit. Mrs. Osborn was dressed top to bottom in her usual black.

Whenever she came to dinner Daddy would always start the conversation by asking her a question so that she'd feel welcome. Ten minutes later she ...maybe ...would have finished answering. We always knew what was coming and, facing the usual boredom of her answers, would think about the coming afternoon and what fun thing we would find to do. Mrs. Osborn spoke as fast as chipmunks squeak and we became fascinated by the fact that the rest of her face never moved to smile or frown; it was only her lips that moved. One particular Sunday, as we ate the main course, Daddy, knowing Mrs. Osborn's love of books, asked her what was the latest book she'd read. She had just put a forkful of salad into her mouth and, of course, had to swallow before answering, but when she began her usual long-winded reply, a piece of lettuce heavily covered with French dressing, had glued itself to her upper lip. I can't remember the name of the book she'd read, but, in the amount of time it took her to answer, we could have read the Encyclopedia Britannica from beginning to end. Flap, flap, flap, went the tiny bit of lettuce—so fast, we were mesmerized. After what seemed days of the lettuce madly flying, Daddy leaned over, pointed his finger towards her lip, and softly said, "Mrs. Osborn." Amazingly, she stopped talking and, squinting down at her lip, took up her napkin and wiped away the piece of lettuce. I don't remember much after that except holding my breath so tightly that I almost choked. To this day, if any member of our various families sees anything—a piece of lettuce, a bit of paper napkin, a crumb of bread—sticking to a family member's lip, that person will point and say, "Mrs. Osborn," and whatever is sticking is automatically wiped away. That day with Mrs. Osborn started out boring but, as often was the case, ended up being one of our favorite Sundays.

Then, there was the lunch when our guest was Morris Frank, founder of the Seeing Eye Organization. Mr. Frank had become Dad's friend and a member of St. Peter's congregation. He, himself, was blind, and as we ate, his friendly guide dog lay peacefully under the table. I was about seven years old and Rob and I were the only kids present. I was sitting across from Mr. Frank and, as usual, Rob began teasing me to the point where I whined, "Stop being so mean!"

Mr. Frank looked across at me and said, "Laird, for a boy, you're acting pretty girly." In the strongest voice I could master, I said, "I am a girl!!"

He let this sink in and replied, "Then, act like a boy and give it to him!" Because my name is Laird—a male's name—people who've heard my name but haven't met me, assume I must be male. As for Rob, I later learned to follow Mr. Frank's advice and "give it to him."

On yet another Sunday, the presiding bishop came to our church to confirm new church members with the "laying on of hands" ceremony. Mother, of course, asked him to lunch. As usual, she had picked out a proper Sunday dress for me, brushed my hair with extra care and sent me off to church to be confirmed. When the designated time came for the confirmees to move to the alter rail, I crept up, scared to death, and knelt down. The bishop came to me and blessed me with his hands on my head. I took the prescribed little wafer—the body of Christ—and put it in my mouth. Then he held the carafe, filled with apple juice, and we all took a sip. I took a hefty swallow and then, to my horror, I let out an ear-splitting belch. Everyone gasped and put their hands over their mouths to keep from laughing. In case I was choking, the bishop gave me a solid pat on the back and then moved on. It took all my strength to stay firmly on my knees, but soon the service was completed and I was free to go home.

At lunch, I was seated next to the bishop. I started eating with my head bent so low in humiliation that the soup almost hit my nose, but then the kind, kind bishop turned to me and said, "You know, Laird, one Sunday back when I was a boy, I knelt down to take communion", and here, he whispers to me, "and made a noise from my other end. Burping is nothing!"

But, the "Five Star" lunch occurred on Thanksgiving Day in 1946, after the war was over. Someone had told Daddy of a local young woman who'd been "Miss March" on one of the Petty Calendars—pinup calendars that featured a bathing-suited babe for each calendar month. These calendars had definitely helped the soldiers get through the war. The war being over, Miss March was out of calendar work and also divorced with an ailing mother needing care. She desperately needed work and so, typically, kind Daddy suggested to Mother that they hire Miss March to be a temporary maid. It didn't take too much kindness on Daddy's part to agree that Miss March, with her flaming red hair, six foot tall body, and boobs that went across the room, would be the perfect maid. Mother was a bit hesitant but, as always, poor Mother had to play minister's wife and comply. So, Miss March arrived the day before Thanksgiving to start work.

In an effort to make Thanksgiving dinner perfect, Mother asked our sweet, Sunday-maid, Ellen Daisy, to instruct Miss March on how the turkey should be prepared and what to do with the vegetable dishes. Ellen told her that the turkey stuffing would be served separately in a bowl, not stuffed inside the turkey as is most often done. She wanted Miss March to be relaxed in her role as a "Thanksgiving maid."

Next morning, on the big day, Mother took Miss March upstairs and fitted her out in a maid's black uniform and white apron for her Sunday-dinner job. Because Miss March was so tall, the uniform barely covered her knees and the medium-size apron's top pushed her breasts almost up to her chin. In this sexy outfit and with her Christmas-red hair, she could have been Miss December, but no matter which month, she would have provided ammunition to any soldier.

Lunchtime arrived and all of us piled into the dining room, lusting for the holiday meal. We sat down and Dad said grace. After a moment, Mother jingled her little silver bell to signal Ellen to bring in the turkey and, as always, put it in front of Dad for carving. There should have been a swinging "Vavoom!" drumbeat because, it wasn't Ellen who walked in—it was Miss March. Holding the turkey platter, she walked through the kitchen's swinging door, her hips rocking side to side, her long beautiful legs very visible under her too-short uniform, her gorgeous red hair bobbing to the rhythm of her walk. Proudly smiling, she placed the turkey in front of Dad and then stood back, waiting to pass the plates. Ellen had brought in the vegetables and stuffing and they were waiting to be served. Daddy lifted up the carving fork and knife and scraping them, one against the other, said "Let's do it!" With that he dramatically cut a large slice down the turkey's stomach. Suddenly we heard a strange crinkling sound and saw Daddy looking down, his mouth gaping. "Ohhhh my," he said, pulling back the meat around the opening. There, staring up at us was a plastic bag filled with greasy, gray turkey guts. Miss March stared down in horror. She'd been told to prep the turkey, but she'd only prepped the outside. After all, the stuffing was being made separately, wasn't it? We all wanted to laugh, but instinctively knowing how humiliated Miss March must be, we didn't. Mother looked at Miss March and quickly said, "Oh, don't worry about it. I can use them" (meaning the guts) "for a soup." Mother had never made a soup from scratch in her life.

Daddy said, "I've always wanted to know what those other parts were." The rest of us just stared and tried desperately not to giggle. Miss March helped with the cooking on another occasion. Mother asked her to fix sliced bananas for our dessert. Miss March did exactly what she'd been told. She brought in the bananas and yes, they were sliced, but unpeeled.

Miss March stayed a week until she finally found a relative to stay with. During that week she cleaned, made beds and told us hilarious stories about her calendar days. We were sad when she left. So, I imagine, was Dad.

We said, "hi" to our churches in times of joy and sadness. Weddings and funerals, Christmas and Easter turned our church into a glorious theater for beautiful events but it didn't stop there. As we got to say "hi" to our friendly churches more and more, they morphed into our own church-theater of "hi" comedy shows, known as "Trowbridge Pranks."

6 PRANKS BE TO GOD

Church was not only the House of God but ours as well, and, it was the number-one stage set for our own comedy productions. I mean, what could be funnier than doing a prank in a place with an ornate altar, stained glass windows and golden organ pipes. Perfect! Some of these pranks were short one-acts, others not so small. Brother Rob was the first to humanize Sunday church services and break some of the usual holy boredom. His prank was small, but it paved the way for more.

When Rob became "$$uccessful," we always teased him about something he'd done in our Morristown church. One Sunday, when it came time for the collection plate to be passed from row to row, Rob put five hundred dollar Monopoly bills under the real bills in the basket as it was passed down the pews. Nobody mentioned it—there were many naughty kids in the congregation—so every Sunday he'd slip in another wad. After a few Sundays of doing this, Mother was forced to get a new Monopoly set—we kids all pretended that we'd, somehow, lost the money. The church staff found out about this weekly prank and figured it must be Bud Mack, a notably "bad boy," who'd done the trick. Dad's assistant casually confronted Bud by saying, "Hey, that Monopoly trick was a good one," but Bud insisted he was innocent and suggested Dad question Rob. Dad did and Rob answered, "Well, you always say that the collection plate never has enough money!"

Dad replied, "You could have given more, but the joke is over!"

Rob was also the source of high-level pranks. One occurred on a Sunday afternoon after Daddy had met with the vestry members in our study. After the meeting, Mother had invited the members to come outside and have drinks on the patio.

It was a lovely day and the sound of ice, tinkling in gin and tonics, blended nicely with the hum of bees on Mother's peonies. Upstairs, dressed in his usual Bat Man costume, Rob, age twelve, and bored, was going down the front hall stairs and peered out of the stairway window that looked down to the patio below. The parishioners were making polite conversation and looked like they might need a little excitement. Rob decided he'd like to join the folks outside. Very quietly, he opened the window, and making sure that his cape was correctly set on his shoulders, he leaped out of the stairway window, arms spread forward. Miraculously, he landed on the edge of the patio. Unbelievably, everyone survived Rob's comic book entrance—even the tray of hors d'oeuvres was intact. Deciding this was not enough, Rob spun around and rolled down the lawn to the applause of the guests. Mother and Dad weren't amused and Rob was sent straight to his room, his Bat Man costume outlawed for two weeks.

Even our Scottish Airedale, Sandy Mcfarland Trowbridge, pranked. We loved dressing her in a cute little apron with a shopping bag around her neck and then sending her uptown to the A&P. She'd go in the door and wander around the aisles sniffing the food and going up to people for a pat. The shoppers thought this was so funny that they'd put pieces of fruit or vegetable—maybe even a candy bar—into the shopping bag. We'd be outside waiting to take her home and eat the candy bars. Once, Sally dressed Sandy in bra and panties and sent her into a church vestry meeting. Then she called Daddy, and in a French accent said, "Françoise has come to see you." Dad had no idea who was calling until Sandy wandered into the meeting. Dad thought this prank a bit too much, yet he often told the story to others. But the very best of all Trowbridge pranks was one that still lives on as Number One in our family memory bank.

At this time, we still lived in Chestnut Hill, and Anne and Sal were attending Miss Hall's School in Pittsfield, Massachusetts. Sal was taking an arts and crafts course as part of her curriculum. One of her assignments was to learn the art of sewing by making a life-size ragdoll, so she made one that was about my five-year-old height, named it Liz and proudly brought it home. The doll had long yellow braids and blue button eyes, just like mine. Sal, of course, had to dress Liz and soon, naked Liz was in one of my dresses, wearing a pair of my socks and shoes.

One Sunday afternoon when Mother was in bed with one of her recurring "bugs," the house wasn't under its usual guard so Sal, Rob, and Anne, decided to have some fun and took Liz, her braids hanging down, across our driveway to the church. Rob and Anne stood at the church entrance below the huge steeple towering above. Then Sal, carrying Liz, climbed the steeple's winding stone stairs until she was at the very top of the tower. There she found a small narrow window that looked down on the driveway below where Anne and Rob were looking up, waiting. Then, she put Liz up to the window ledge and wobbled her back and forth. Seeing Liz, Anne and Rob immediately began to shout, "Laird. Don't jump! Don't jump! We won't be mean to you anymore!" At this point Sal heaved "me" out of the window and, with braids and arms outspread, I plummeted toward my death. Luckily, Anne and Rob caught and saved me. I attempted suicide three times that afternoon. Daddy found out and trying to stifle a laugh, told them not to do this anymore, that it wasn't funny at all and the "church is not a place for tricks." Oh, really?

They stopped my suicides attempts that day, but not forever. During vacation times when we were all at home, they took place quite often. One Saturday morning, when Daddy was in his church office editing tomorrow's sermon, a member of the congregation was driving down Hammond Street, opposite the church. To his horror, he saw the Preacher's Kid, Laird, hurtling off the church tower.

Because of a tall row of bushes near the road, he couldn't see Anne and Rob, only Laird, flying through the air. Racing his car into the driveway that led to the back of the church, he rushed into Dad's office, and with gasps of horror and outstretched hands, he screamed, "Reverend Trowbridge ... something ... terrible ... has happened!" Apparently, Dad flicked his cigarette ashes into his ashtray, casually lifted his head, and smiling, said, "Oh, did they throw that doll off again?"

Liz lived on and, having died by suicide, was resurrected by being given a pair of white feathery wings, a white angel robe, and a large golden halo. She sat on the top of Sally's grandfather clock for years. The last time I saw her was at the wedding of Sal's daughter, Peggy, held at the old Chestnut Hill church where Liz had been born. There she was, wings and all, sitting on a table, greeting the wedding guests as they came in. They'd all heard the story, so were happy to see their friend. Liz now lives with Peggy—I suspect she will live a long, long life.

Still living in Chestnut Hill, my siblings did a Halloween prank that almost hit the front page of the local newspaper. Around midnight, Sal, Anne and Rob, then at local schools and living at home, did a prank they'd planned for days. Sneaking into the church basement in the middle of the night, they took several packing ropes; tied them together and attached a bunch of tin cans from our trashcan. When the job was done, they tiptoed out to Hammond Street, carefully strung the ropes between two small trees on either side of the street, and waited. Being very late, there were very few cars passing by, but after a few minutes a car slowly came down the street, banged into the tin cans and screeched to a stop. The fenders of the car had been snagged in the rope and the tin cans were stuck in the car's axle. Someone got out with a flashlight and was trying to undo the ropes when another car came up the street and stopped to help. The man trying to unleash his car was the town mayor. The woman on the passenger side was not the mayor's wife. The woman was Miss $$omebody Else. Word got all around town. No one ever knew who'd done the Halloween trick. After all, it was Halloween, wasn't it? Kids all over town were doing tons of pranks—weren't they?

When we moved to Morristown, and Dad became minister of St. Peter's Church, the church pranks didn't die. I was so lonely for the past—especially Tony—and frightened by my future in a new town and a new school that, for the first and only time in my life I gained a hefty amount of weight by feeding my cavern of loneliness with cookies. I became so chubby that my new classmates called me "Lard" or "Sideways." "Sideways" was born from the fact that my chubby self had to slip sideways into my L-shaped desk instead of sliding easily into the front opening. When the kids called me "Sideways" they'd double up with laughter, but one girl didn't and would tell them to stop. That girl was my classmate, Mary Treat Nettleton. She was tall, with short red hair and freckles and usually wore a plaid skirt and sweater buttoned down the back. To my delight, Mary Treat had a sense of humor and because her family attended our church, we soon were making faces and playing a long-distance version of Rock, Paper, Scissors across the aisle from each other. Church had become fun again. One Sunday, the organist started the processional with a chord that could have leveled the pews, maybe the whole town. This inspired us, and after church we met and came up with a plan—some Saturday night we'd stuff the organ pipes with toilet paper and Kleenex. If we were lucky, maybe the "stuff" would muffle the next morning's organ sounds. We decided this would be "real neat," so the next Saturday night, armed with our soft white ammunition, we snuck into the church through a secret door I knew of, and with flashlight in hand, spent a good hour stuffing the organ pipes that bordered the chancel in front of the altar. The openings in the organ pipes were deep enough so that no one would be able to see the white tissues on Sunday.

The next morning, Mary Treat and I came to church with our families and sat in our regular pews across from each other, all dressed up and ready to pray. We could see the organist sitting quietly in his nook, his hands ready to play the processional. Suddenly, his arms raised and then slammed down on the keys. The church exploded with an ear-splitting chord and, ta da, the apse was filled with puff-puffs of white fluff. For a second there was silence and then you could hear gasps everywhere. Mary Treat and I looked at each other, and with our hands over our mouths, gasped, "Oh my God! Who did THAT?" The choir members rushed out of their stalls and for a good ten minutes the congregation, bent over in laughter, watched the cleanup. Because other prankish kids attended Sunday services and I was "the minister's daughter" who would *never* do such a thing, we weren't even suspected. Mary Treat and I had become best friends and realized that we definitely were a good team with talent for tricks, and the most outrageous was soon to come.

One beautiful Easter Sunday, when the church was alight with Easter lilies, Mary Treat came by my house to chat before the service. We were dressed in our Easter best—pleated skirts, blouses with Peter Pan collars, and, of course, Mary Jane shoes.

Upstairs in my bedroom, looking out the window, we chatted about our usual subject of conversation—boys. From the window, we could see the old church graveyard that spread directly below and reached across to the side of the church. We also talked about the amazing, (believable?) Easter story about Jesus' resurrection. There, below us, were very old graves. Had all those dead people gone to heaven? What if they were only bones in boxes? Could we work on this? Mary and I looked at each other and went downstairs.

The graves closest to the sidewalk were ancient "table graves," ones with stone legs and slabs on top. Their inscriptions were carved on the slabs and there was enough space between the slabs and the earth to, yes, accommodate a real, live body. It was early enough so that the churchgoers hadn't started to park and weren't yet walking down the sidewalk to attend the service. This allowed us to casually edge our way across the graveyard, pretending to read the names on the gravestones until we found two fairly tall table graves. Making sure no one was around, we squeezed under. Looking sideways at each other, we nodded in silent agreement and then slowly crossed our arms over our chests like the dead in open caskets. Trying not to slap at curious ants, we waited.

Eventually, we began to hear the clip, clop of peoples' shiny Easter shoes walking toward the church. After we were confident that the sidewalk was filled with people, we nodded an "OK" to each other, quickly twisted our bodies out from beneath the graves and, with our arms raised to heaven, shouted "Ta Da!" Like Jesus—we had resurrected. The walkers stopped in amazement. There were gasps of horror but then, thank God, there were irreligious roars of laughter. This prank was the best, but not the best for us. After hearing about our resurrection, Daddy scolded me strongly and banished me to my room for the rest of Easter Sunday. No ham, no mashed potatoes, no asparagus with Hollandaise Sauce. Mary Treat's parents did the same.

As we got older and were finishing up at Peck School, Mary Treat and I stopped our church pranks. We did naughty things at school—leading necking parties in the upstairs bathroom; writing phony love letters from handsome Ned Langhorne or Freddy Thorne, which we dropped on girls' desks; pretending we'd twisted our ankles on the playing field so that our gorgeous male athletic teacher would take us inside and wrap bandages around a "very painful" foot or... better yet... our knee. And then something happened which changed our outlook forever.

One of our classmates, Priscilla Mutch, whose father was the Presbyterian minister in town, had struggled with results of early polio for all the years we'd known her. Although she always limped, she, remarkably, did special exercises which helped her do most activities. She had a good sense of humor and was friendly and warm. During the summer of our senior year, Priscilla had improved so much that she was able to do something she'd always dreamed of doing— water ski. One day she did it successfully and had great fun but to our horror, she caught a cold which turned into pneumonia. We knew she was very sick, but people recovered from pneumonia, didn't they? The school administration sent flowers from her class so that she would know that each classmate was thinking of her. But, as time went on, Priscilla was not back in school. And then, a week later, our principal called us into a meeting and told us the unbelievably sad news that Priscilla had died. To have a classmate die at such a young age—our age—introduced us, for the first time, to the concept of the fragility of life. Hers was my first "funeral." Mary Treat and I looked at each other across the aisle with tears in our eyes. From then on whenever things got tough at home or school, I would think of Priscilla and be inspired by her courageous resilience. We were now a bit more grown up and life wasn't centered around doing funny things. We, intuitively, realized that church-pranking might be something done by young kids and maybe—just maybe— Laird and Mary Treat were too old for that sort of thing? We were and we stopped.

Even though church-pranking stopped, pranking at home continued, especially at Green Pastures, our real, live, Trowbridge home.

Liz Lives On

7 GREEN PASTURES

The House

My strong emotional attachment to Green Pastures became very clear one day, when I was thirty, and living in Princeton, New Jersey. A good friend told me she'd been to a "fascinating" young female psychic living outside of town and, knowing that I was a sucker for all mysterious happenings, suggested I go. She assured me that this psychic was not a fake; she had been a sane, serious high school teacher and, most importantly, charged very little. Apparently, she had acknowledged her gift of unusual insight, left her teaching job and now, along with taking care of her own children, had set up shop. So, one day we went. Though I was reasonably suspicious, I knew that—if nothing else—what happened would be entertaining. Little did I know. When we arrived, a pretty young woman greeted us at the door and asked us to come in. This was Nancy, the psychic, and her natural, friendly smile told me she wasn't acting. She quickly took me into a cozy room, sat me in a comfortable chair across from her and began to chat.

"You smoke, don't you?" she asked. I guessed that I reeked from Kent cigarette smoke.

"Yes," I answered, "too much."

She ignored that and pointing to a place behind her shoulder, said, "You have a pain right here don't you? "

"Yes," I said. "I've had it all my life." She paused and asked, "Have you been to the Southwest or, if not, would you like to go?" I admitted that I'd never been and, strangely, the thought of it was unappealing. "In fact," I said, "I really don't want to go at all!"

She looked at me and said, "The reason you don't want to go, Laird, is because, in your former life, you were a cowboy sitting on a horse, smoking a cigarette, and a Native American shot you in the back with an arrow!" I gasped in disbelief. Could this explanation of my back pain be true in any way? Don't most people have a pain somewhere in their backs?

We sat there for a few silent moments and then she looked straight into my eyes and said, "I'm feeling that there's a very, very important place in your life with a ... a biblical name?" I was so astonished I couldn't do anything but shake my head in disbelief.

"Yes," I gasped. "There's a place that means more to me than any other place I know." I told her about our family's summer place in New Hampshire.

"It's called Green Pastures," I said, "as in the biblical psalm, 'He maketh me lie down in green pastures.'"

At the end of our session Nancy gave me a tape of our whole conversation. I have that tape and to this day it is still true. Green Pastures was, and is, a marquee headline in my life. I left the psychic's house a believer in her powers. And I still believe.

The Green Pastures story begins back in the summer of 1929 when my parents went on their usual vacation to Hancock Point, Maine, to be with Dad's parents and his brother and sister at their summer home. Because of the din of his siblings and the usual familial tensions, it was no vacation. It got to the point that Dad told his father he wanted to find a place of his own and his father offered him five thousand dollars to buy a house. Having heard from some friends that there was a house on a large tract of land near Harrisville, New Hampshire, Dad and Mother were curious, so in January 1930, on snowshoes and suffering four feet of snow, they had their first sight of their future summer home. They slept that night in sleeping bags while mice crawled over and around them—a bizarre welcome to what would come to be their beautifully decorated and homey home.

A farmer had built the house in 1790 along with a massive barn that had housed oxen for hauling logs and plowing. Later on, it had been owned by a Mr. and Mrs. Rolfe—Mr. Rolfe being a descendant of the one and only John Rolfe who'd married Pocahontas. They'd "done over" the house badly, but the barn was beautifully restored during their attempt to run a summer camp for girls interested in Shakespearean plays. This had not been successful due to the girls not being allowed to swim in nearby, beautiful, Silver Lake, and also because they had to wear their Shakespearean costumes, not just on stage, but all day. My parents bought the place and the surrounding 200 acres for forty-five hundred dollars. They named this new, summer haven Green Pastures—partly to echo Psalm 23, but mostly because of the actual green pastures that looked out on a beautiful view of Mount Monadnock. A treacherous dirt road, only travelled during the summers, ran by the house and barn, then up a steeply curving hill towards the small town of Nelson. In the eighteenth century the oxen would come down this steep hill, plod their way through the barn's massive bottom door, trudge up a circular ramp to the main level where they would go to their stalls, put their heads out of low doors to a trough, filled with edible hay. They would sleep in these open stalls—as we did more than a hundred years later.

The Bat's Barn

Our family stayed at Green Pasture from mid-June until just after Labor Day when school started. The long summer vacation was possible as Dad was given the summer off to write his next year's sermons, thereby allowing his assistant to experience being a chaplain for the summer. Out in the backwoods there was a one-room hut where Dad would go each day to do his work. It was forbidden to us, but the house, the barn, the fields, and the road were ours.

From the very start Green Pastures became Mother's adopted baby. Using her decorator talents, she dressed it in special clothes, polished its body with deeply fragrant oil, diapered its bare bottom with updated plumbing. With the help of her black Singer sewing machine, she toiled through endless nights to make everything this re-born house needed. When I spent my first summer there, she'd spent years working on the house and barn, and pictures from that time show them, colorful and perfectly done.

The house was a typical wood-shingled colonial home with a small living room, dining room, and kitchen downstairs. At the top of ancient, narrow stairs were three bedrooms and a bath. We children became so bonded with the rooms of the house that years later, one of us could ask, "Remember the pillows on the living room couch?" and immediately the answer would come back, "You mean those big green, orange, and beige ones?" I can still see mother's light green chaise with her little woven blanket at its end. She would sit there painting her nails Rose Red while Dad read to us in his upholstered dark green armchair to the left of the fireplace. At one end of the living room, the wood floor was bisected by a different colored floorboard going across the room. This marked where the original main room had ended and another, called, "the birthing room" had begun. Here the babies were born and slept until old enough to be moved upstairs.

The upstairs bathroom is etched in my memory. It wasn't a room as much as it was a small attic space under the roof's peak, a space that contained cartons of junk, an old toilet and sink, and one dim wall light. The primary users of this space were bats so, naturally, we called it the Bat Room. Inside the entry door, Mother had hung a tennis racket, just in case you needed to swat a bat before sitting on the john. None of us liked bats, but Dad was known for being absolutely terrified of them. Dad was also known for sleepwalking.

One unforgettable night he walked down the hall— asleep—to take a leak; opened the Bat Room door and was hit in the face by a gigantic, flapping bat. Mother heard a loud thumping noise and ran out of their bedroom to find her "Corny" hunched at the top of the stairs next to the Bat Room with a bat somehow attached to his pajama bottoms.

Mother, always gutsy, slapped at Dad's pants and freed the bat. We, sleeping in the barn, only heard about this happening later but from then on the phrase, "bat in the belfry" became "bat in the belt, free."

The bats' main home, though, was the barn, twice as wide as the house and rising three stories high to massive beams under its peaked roof. At night we used to play a record of Dick Haymes singing "It's a Grand Night for Singing" on the old record player and the bats would suddenly fly. We figured there must have been one note that irritated or pleased them that, when reached, made them swoop down and across the large barn expanse. In anticipation, we were armed with tennis rackets to begin our usual "bat hunt." Needless to say, Dad never joined in.

One night, Mother and Dad had invited a couple to play bridge and the four of them were seated at a small card table by the house's windows that could be seen from the barn. I was about eight and Rob twelve and after our "bat hunt" yielded a dead bat, Rob said to Anne, Sal, and me, "I have a great idea!" He then proceeded to put the bat into his pants pocket and signaled us to follow him toward the house. We came to a spot where we were able to see the bridge players up the rise and through the window. Rob instructed us to wait. Then we watched him casually enter the house and, in a moment, saw him standing next to Dad who was seated at the table, facing us from above.

Dad and Mother were notorious smokers and, as usual, a pack of Camels was at the ready by Dad's left hand. Rob politely greeted the guests with a smile and made some pleasant small talk and then, to our horror, surreptitiously slipped Dad's cigarette pack off the table, and casually walked away. In a few seconds he returned and replaced the cigarette pack next to Dad's elbow. After some more small talk, Rob left the house and joined us at the bottom of the rise where we'd watched the whole drama.

After a moment, Dad reached for his Camels and pulled out what he thought was a smoke. There—in his hand— was the dead bat. In a flash, the table lifted, spun around, and cards flew through space while the bridge players leaped around the room in terror. We all dashed back to the barn and waited for Dad to come tearing down to ream us out. In a minute he came, stomping through the rollback door to the back where we were huddled waiting for the worst. He came to us and in a controlled voice said, "Rob...if...you... ever...do...that...again...I'll...make...you...eat...the...bat! He meant it and we never played with a bat again.

The living room was the main room of our Green Pastures life. We would lie on the long—what we called—"ship couch," and with our arms, paddle our hands by its sides. But when Dad read aloud to us, we were quiet, entranced with his Gregory Peck voice, interrupted now and then with the sound of his sipping the bourbon and soda always on the table by his side. After going for a refill, he would stop in the hallway out of our sight, then he'd edge his hand around the door and claw at the wall to frighten us. He never did, he only brought giggles. We were never bored, as one week he'd read us Dickens and the next a Saturday Evening Post mystery— he, again, the beloved star, and we, the audience.

The dining room was also a place of fun. Because "G.P"— as we called Green Pastures—was our home-away-from-church, Dad's summer grace was "Good food, good meat. Good God, let's eat!" We loved it. Mother would raise her eyes to heaven in disapproval. We'd sit and "dine" at a long wooden table in the room alongside the farmer's fireplace. One night, Mother, the world's most terrible cook, had brought in our tasteless chicken and mashed potatoes. As we were madly slurping milk to wash down the meal, Dad started telling us about when he was a teenager and the times he'd spent with his father in Europe climbing in the Alps. One of us asked, "How were you ever able to climb those huge mountains when you were so young?" Without a thought, he got up, went to the wall and said, "Like this." Before we knew it, he'd put his right foot on top of an old iron brad that stuck out from the wall. Back in the 1800's, it had been used for holding metal pots, but now the brad was the first level of his mountain climb. Next, he'd grabbed the fireplace mantle and swung his leg over to a higher brad and then, to our amazement, he was totally stretched out, reaching toward the old candle chandelier on the ceiling. Mother was screaming "Stop! Don't!" and laughing, he swung back down. "See?" he said, "It's not so hard". We sat, our mouths agape, but now we knew.

The kitchen was mostly Mother's. It still had its original small black wood stove, but next to it was a 1940s "modern" stovetop. At night our job was to periodically fill the side stove with wood, and to set the table and wipe up spills on the wood counters. After dinner we would clear the table, Dad would wash the dishes in the old stone sink. We'd dry, and all of us would harmonize funny songs, like "My Father Killed a Kangaroo. *That—* was a terrible thing to do" and finally troop into the living room. Dad would read aloud to us and then (if I was old enough to stay up as late as my siblings) we'd walk down the ancient stone steps to the barn where—if the bats weren't flapping—we'd sleep.

The old barn was a live-in arena with an enormous fireplace at one end and a triangular balcony at the other. The huge main area of the barn had a ping pong table in the center. When we had large parties, the ping pong table was home for the h'ors d'oeuvres, corner ashtrays and cocktail napkins. At small parties, guests would inevitably play a game—ping pong paddle in one hand, a drink in the other. At the rear of the barn was a wide sliding door which opened to large back fields. Directly below, at ground level, was an ancient bathroom with a sink looking out to the fields.

One morning I was in the downstairs bathroom brushing my teeth. Looking out the window to the fields above, I saw Mother walking up toward the house with a large scruffy looking...oh-my-god...bobcat behind her. She obviously knew it was there as she beckoned it with her hand, calling "Here, kitty, kitty. Here, kitty, kitty." I was terrified, but to my amazement, I saw this beast was quietly trailing along and eventually, they drifted behind the house. I ran up to the house, sure that I'd find Mother lying, half eaten, in the field. When I got there, the bobcat was out back, happily lying in the tall grass. Staring out the back window, I saw Mother emerge from the kitchen tossing our morning Cheerios toward him. The bobcat slowly got up and, as if to say "thanks," looked at Mother and sniffed his way toward the food. When he'd finished, he looked back at her and as if to say "goodbye," headed out across the field toward the woods.

Terrified, I rushed out screaming at Mother, "Get back! Get back inside!"

Mother, still looking at the disappearing bobcat, turned and casually said, "He's not dangerous. He's old." Mother could be very empathetic when she wanted to be.

At times when work was being done on our downstairs bedroom ox stalls, we kids were made to use the barn's three rooms that arched along the barn's balcony. The rooms also had no ceilings. Not only did we have to listen to the swish of the carousing nighttime bats—so close to us now—but we also had to deal with huge, black, fuzzy spiders that lived on the beams above. Years later, I wrote the following poem about how laughter was our way of conquering fear.

Fact of Spiders

At nap time,
under the roof-fall
of the renovated ox barn,
we lay on narrow iron cots,
in our ox stall "rooms,"
ceilinged by beams alone and shot
the giant dust ball spiders
—up above—
with brightly colored rubber bands,
giggling up bravado through it all.

At night time, in the thickened dark,
we knew the plum-size beasts were there,
parachuting down on silken threads,
their aim to burrow up beneath our spreads,
hungry to scuttle through our hair.

On nights too still,
we slapped our palms against the pine-planked walls,
imitating flanks of spiders stalking, leg, by leg, by leg.
Belly-crazed with laughter,
we pounded out our code of bravery,
until exhausted,
we gave way to sleepy bed.

Only rain, drumming on the shingled roof,
or wind, rattling the seeded window panes,
lightning cracks, so welcome, sweet,
and mutinous claps of thunder,
ever covered up the threat of lumbering spider feet.

To this day
there are tattered rings of green
and red and yellow rubber missiles
clinging to the rafters
where we shot at hovering fear,
trying to make something funny
out of something that was not.
We did it well.
We did it well into our years.

It was easy to make "something funny" out of the spider-
nights because those nights were nights my siblings and I
were together, but it was not funny when I had to spend

nights in the barn alone. From the age of six, I was considered old enough to sleep in one of the stalls in the barn, but being so much younger than my siblings, I was made to go to bed much earlier than they. Dad would read aloud to us in the living room and Mother would nod, point to me and say "Laird, bedtime." It was as if she were identifying a murderess in a police lineup. Sally, being kind, would grab her flashlight and lead me down the bumpy stone steps to the barn. She would take me into my stall, light the kerosene lamp and help me into my pajamas. Then, when I was in bed, she'd kiss me goodnight and turn off the lamp. I could hear her steps fading as she walked back up the stone steps to the house. Then, I'd be alone in the deafening quiet. I'd lie facing the wall that separated my stall from Anne and Sal's rooms (they had ceilings!) and start whispering to myself and an imaginary friend, asking the friend questions and answering myself. I had a flashlight for walking downstairs to the bathroom (something I would only do when the others came to bed) but to turn it on now would arouse the waiting bats hanging from the barn's ceiling. Inevitably, I would hear the flap of their wings as they started to fly. Perhaps my whispering had woken them, or perhaps they'd been waiting just for me? Once they'd started their nighttime swoop, I'd hide under the covers. Even so, my imagination was in high gear and I could see them in my mind's eye flapping above me—dipping and swooping down closer and closer to my bed.

One night, one did. As usual, I was lying on my left side, facing Sal's room and, to my horror, I heard a swish and flap above my head and then a loud thump on the wall. Another thump and I knew a bat was stuck in my stall. I pulled the covers over my head and lay without moving an inch, praying it would fly up and out, but no luck. It kept flapping and hitting the walls for what seemed hours, until, finally, it stopped. I didn't dare move in case it was just resting, but my body was so tense from lying absolutely still that I had to move. I turned and took my Eveready flashlight and swept its beam around the room. There, on the floor right beside my bed was the bat—dead. He must have lost his radar and hit the wall too hard. He was so close to my bed that, if I'd gotten out without my flashlight, I would have stepped on him. No matter, I had to get this sci-fi creature out of my room. So, I reached down, pinched his wing and swung him up onto the bedside table. My flashlight beamed down on its staring, beady eyes, its devil fangs. With my heart thumping and thinking that maybe it's just knocked out, I took it by its wing and rushed to the

Dutch door, opened the top and threw it as far as I could. Then I crawled over the top of the door, and stumbled my way up the stone stairs to the back door of the house. Dad was still in his chair, reading aloud; mother was crocheting; and Rob, Anne, and Sal were lying on the sofa. I stomped into the living room and, standing as tall as I could, loudly announced, "A bat died in my room. I am NEVER going to sleep alone in that barn again!"

Dad stopped reading and looked at me, his eyes wide with wonder and with understanding. "Okay, Laird. You never have to."

Mother stared at me, and knowing that I'd meant it said, "Well, I guess that's it."

Finally, I was my own person, free from that nighttime prison. When I was old enough to stay up as late as my siblings, we would go down to the barn together. In the meantime, I was allowed to sleep in the house. However, to this day, when I am alone in a silent, large room, I can still hear those bats in the barn. When I'm home, I turn the TV or radio down low for background noise. I absolutely adore the sound of thunder, wind, and rain, welcome substitutes for the sound of bats.

Happily, the barn was not only a home for scary bats; it was often the stage for large, loud, and funny barn parties.

Birthday parties, anniversaries, and Fourth of July parties gave us the chance to sing in front of the huge fireplace and, inevitably, make people laugh. Accompanying the songs and laughter was quite a bit of booze—though no wine—just bourbon, beer, scotch and the expected gin martinis. We kids thought it hysterically funny to watch the guests get "tiddly", or "in their cups" as my parents called it. Sometimes, a guest would get blasted, always politely, but blasted nonetheless.

During one typical summer party, the barn was abuzz with guests. Sunlight streamed through the windows, transforming the barn into a stage for this afternoon's party. I was standing next to Mother and one of our good friends, Robb Sagendorph, who lived in a lakeside house down the road, in the town of Dublin. Mr. Sagendorph, had become editor of The Old Farmer's Almanac in the thirties. He looked exactly like Abe Lincoln. The first time I met him was on a Labor Day. He didn't say hello. Instead, in a strong New England accent, he said "Summah's most ovah, go roll in the clovah." Needless to say, he was a character.

At this party, Mother and he were chatting away when he reached for his drink. Forgetting he'd put it on the window sill, he stretched up his arm to a reachable beam where he'd spotted a glass. Thinking it was his bourbon and soda, he took a big swig, and to my horror, immediately spat it out, all over the person next to him. It was then that Mother, the constant gardener, said in a low voice, "Oh dear. That glass was filled earlier with flowers for the party." Mr. Sagendorph had swigged down peony and petunia piss! Thankfully, "Abe Lincoln" thought it hysterically funny and lived to tell the tale—many times.

At the same party something else happened which was funny at the time, but could have resulted in disaster. At the rear of the barn were sliding doors that opened out to the fields beyond. Facing the doors was a long table lined with bottles of booze that sat alongside a bottle of ginger ale and a pitcher of water—barely touched. We'd hired one of the neighbor's sons to tend bar. He knew everyone there, so he'd joke with them which, of course, resulted in making them stay longer and drink more.

Dad and a good friend, Mr. Thorpe, were at the back door talking and laughing. Dad had a martini in hand and Mr. Thorpe held a scotch and water. Occasionally, Dad gave Mr. Thorpe a light arm-punch to punctuate a funny remark and their heads bent as they roared with laughter— *not* expected behavior for a minister—but, then, this was vacation time. After a few moments, the two of them moved to the sliding door and stood, drinks in hand. Dad leaned out and pointed to the grassy fields across the way. Looking at them, I imagined that he was telling Mr. Thorpe the story about Mother leading the bobcat to the woods behind the house. Suddenly, I saw the two of them slowly roll out of the back door and disappear. I, and others who'd seen this, ran to see what had happened. We could see nothing but fields in front of us, but then, to our right, we heard a noise. There, down a five-foot bank, lay Dad and Mr. Thorpe, laughing, their eyes wide open, their legs straight up against the sides of the bank. Unbelievably, their drinks were still in their hands—a highball glass for Mr. Thorpe and a crystal martini glass for Dad. They'd gone outside to see the fields, had slipped on the side of the bank and slowly slid down. They were lucky!

Parties in the barn were fun but not as important as the tennis court down the road. Dad was King of the Court; so good a player that he'd once played with Alice Marble who, in the thirties, won 12 U.S. Opens and 5 Wimbledon titles. To the world's amazement—Dad won. The court was his other child, and being family, it became a very good friend to us all. During weekends, it was the most important place of all.

Mother didn't play tennis, and one day while all of us were at the tennis court, she had a terrifying experience.

Because our guest players were coming to the house for after-tennis drinks, she busied herself with tidying up the living room. Alongside the room's colonial fireplace was a low door that opened into a wood closet. Mother went to get a log for a possibly chilly night fire and when she pulled it out, a long, long snake wrapped itself around one of her legs and clung to her without moving. She wasn't sure if it was just a garter snake or, God forbid, a poisonous timber rattler, so there was nothing for her to do but stand totally still until the monster chose to move on—but it didn't. When the tennis group finally came to the house, they found Mother standing, holding onto the log of wood. She was as rigid as an obelisk, white as a sheet. In a whisper, she said, "Help! My leg!" Dad looked at the snake and, luckily knowing it was a garter snake, pried it off with a fireplace poker at which point Mother fell on the couch, crying from exhaustion and fear. The next day Dad brought us a book about Northeastern snakes and we were made to memorize the looks of every poisonous snake.

On Labor Day, the holiest tennis day of the year, Mother was usually pouring iced tea up at the court as everyone got ready for the game of the summer. Dad, Rob and Bill Eustis, the son of close family friends and about Anne's age, were the usual male players; Anne and Sal, comprised the female team, but on Labor Day they switched it up—the males dressed as females, the females as males. Dad and Bill would wear fluffy skirts and huge flowered hats and Sal and Anne wore shirts and ties (one summer Bill made huge diapers out of towels and became a baby who played tennis.) Both sides would yell to each other, Dad and Bill in high female voices and Sal and Anne in male growls. It didn't matter what the score was—it was great vaudeville.

When I think of the tennis court I always think of Bill, whose parents lived near us in Chestnut Hill and in the summer, just down the road from Green Pastures. He was not only a great tennis player, but could have doubled for sexy Cary Grant. His athletic body and humorous mind made him the Trowbridge girls' idol. He was often on our court playing tennis or in the barn firing a ping pong ball to victory.

During WWII, Bill gave up tennis and became an air force pilot. One day his parents received a letter with the devastating news of Bill's death. The letter told them that Bill's plane had been shot down off the coast of Japan. Apparently, there were many searches, but neither he nor his plane were found. Our New Hampshire life was no longer the same.

Six months after his death when the war had finally ended, Mother was reading an article in the Boston Herald about the discovery of a Japanese prison camp and a list of the prisoners who'd been found and were on their way home. One of the prisoner's names was a William Eustis from Chestnut Hill, Mississippi. Mother, wisely, did not say a word of this to Bill's parents, but instead called Massachusetts Senator, Henry Cabot Lodge, a personal friend through Dad's Boston church work. The likelihood of there being a Bill Eustis from Chestnut Hill, Massachusetts and one from Chestnut Hill, Mississippi, was too blatantly slim to overlook. Senator Lodge did research and confirmed what Mother had suspected—there was no Chestnut Hill, Mississippi. Sure enough it was Bill. His plane had been shot down near to a Japanese beach, allowing him to swim ashore. He was found there by some children who quickly reported him to the Army station. His long, torturous, incarceration began.

Bill, weighing a little over a hundred pounds, spent time recovering in a Boston hospital and afterward made his triumphal return to his New Hampshire home not far from Green Pastures. His parents had raised the American flag from half-mast to its celebratory height and a welcome home party was given in Bill's honor. Though his mother had prepared a special dinner—barbequed roast pork—Bill couldn't eat a bite. Bent over, he walked as far away from the barbeque pit as he could. We were told later that as a prisoner, he was often forced to eat pieces of rotting pork in lieu of going without food. Bill only ate vegetables that night, but he was smiling.

Despite Bill's horrifying war experience, he soon became the beloved Bill we had known all those years before the war. As usual, my sister Sal had a great idea. Every summer on the date of Bill's homecoming we would have a "Resurrection Day" party in the barn. Having been Angel Gabriel in the church Christmas Eve production, she knew everything about making angel wings and halos. With bendable wire and white cloth covered with paper feathers, she made a huge pair of wings and an accompanying golden halo for Bill to wear. Every successive year until Bill married and spent his summers elsewhere, we celebrated Resurrection Day in the barn filled from end to end with Bill's friends and family. Despite this angelic, feminine costume, Bill still looked like Cary Grant—now with wings. With a drink in one hand and a cigarette in the other, he made heaven look like a real bash.

Bill—our angel

As I and my siblings got older, Green Pastures remained an important part of our lives. In our thirties, we continued to go there for at least a visit. When our parents were too old to make the trip, Rob, Sal, Anne and I would alternate weekend visits. We'd bring friends and tell old Green Pastures stories of tennis, swimming, our laughing, and bats. One weekend visit, when my husband, Reid, and I were living in New York, we invited some friends up for the weekend. We had found a fake bat in a toy store and brought it with us. Needless to say, I told our guests the history of bat-life in the barn, and while we were having dinner, Reid sneaked down to the barn and clamped the bat onto a lampshade in the main room. He then turned on the lamp's light and the bat's scary silhouette was so pronounced, it could even be seen from the front door. After dinner, Reid suggested we go to the barn and have a hot game of ping pong. On walking into the barn, one of the quests saw the bat, ran to a tennis racket on the couch, picked it up and raced over to the lamp, and to save us all—smashed the bat on the shade. The lamp crashed to the floor, broke in pieces and in the middle of the mess was "the bat"—dead. The guest raised his hands in triumph and we doubled over in hysterics. For me, humor had won The Battle of the Bulge of Bats in the Barn.

One year, Mother announced that she couldn't take another summer at Green Pastures (too much entertaining) so she and Dad rented a house on Chappaquiddick Island, near Edgartown, Massachusetts. It was a nice little two story house right by the beach. The beach-front rooms had wide windows so that you could see the whole bay. As you looked out to the water, you saw a little tongue of land that jutted out on the right side of the bay. It had low, flat-roofed brown buildings but they didn't interrupt the beauty of the scene.

The summer we rented this house, Anne and Sal were nineteen and seventeen with beautiful figures and their room was on the bay side of the house. As nothing but water and sand was outside their large window, they rarely pulled their shades down. At night, after a shower, they'd stand, nude, in front of the window and rub their wet heads with bath towels. They thought nothing of it until one morning when they thought a lot about it.

The spit of land that jutted out was home to a Marine training camp. That morning we were getting dressed for breakfast and suddenly heard a long, steady, growling noise outside our window. Mother went to look and quietly said, "The Marines have landed." To our amazement, there—on our beach—was a Marine assault vehicle used for beach battles. They'd come to see Anne and Sal, figuring they'd even look good dressed. Dad went out and yelled "Get the hell off this beach!" and they did, but they left with salutes and big smiles.

We spent one other summer in Nantucket, where we rented a small house on Liberty Street—not on the water— but opposite a small police station. One night, we were woken up by Mother, who said, "Come to the window. You've gotta see this!" We all went to the front door window, peered out at the station and saw—Daddy!— taking a leak right under the street lamp on the station's lawn. He'd thought he was in Green Pastures and had sleepwalked in the direction he always took to go to the "bat room." Luckily, nobody saw him and after finishing his "job" he turned and, in his dream, walked back to his bedroom in Green Pastures.

During that summer, I met lots of young people but somehow missed meeting a boy named, Reid White, who worked pumping gas at the downtown gas station. I was spending most of my time sneaking out to beach parties with the "older crowd." Our main occupation was necking at pretend soccer games. Years later, after Reid and I moved into his family's home in Nantucket, I found that our neighbor's wife was one of my good, old necking buddies. We had many laughs.

I keep a picture of Green pastures in my office. In the picture, Sal, Rob, and I are standing in front of the barn with its huge ox yoke hanging from the top of the wide entrance door. Sally is in the center and we are all smiling at her. Because I was so much younger than my siblings, the time we spent at Green Pastures was the only time I really got to know them. Despite typical sibling conflicts, I think of them often and with love.

Sadly, Green Pasture's life came to a too early end. Rob married Lorna Sagendorph, the daughter of Robb Sagendorph, our Abe Lincoln friend. Lorna was bright and talented and she and Rob lived in nearby Dublin. In the mid

1960s, Mother and Dad told us they couldn't afford to maintain Green Pastures anymore, and gave it to Rob "in lieu of an inheritance." My sisters and I were very surprised, as we'd had no idea that there was any inheritance to be had. In the sixties Rob became publisher of Yankee Magazine and was a New Hampshire State Senator as well as head of its finance committee. He was appointed to take over management of Dad and Mother's finances as well as Green Pastures. Unfortunately, he hired some bad brokers who lost a great deal of our family money. Later, he made up for what they'd lost, but our designated inheritances were greatly diminished.

When Rob owned Green Pastures, he would let us come to visit and bring our young children, but it was no longer a yearly happening. On one visit, Reid and I had brought our two daughters, Gillian and Emilie, and during our visit, I found a tiny wooden doll's bureau that had been mine as a child. I asked to take it home for our kids but Rob said, "Everything in Green Pastures stays in Green Pastures." Needless to say, this was quite hard to take or understand and Reid, the kids and I left—with the bureau. Again, Rob had played King.

Rob rented the property, but after a time, he sold it. The land and lake front went one way, and the house another.

The owners of the house were hippies and let the house fall into dreadful disrepair. It had been my favorite place in the world, and I always had a dream of buying it back. Years later, when I was traveling in New Hampshire, I wanted to drive down the old dirt road and see the house and barn. Rob's son, Jamie, said, "Laird, don't ever go there. It'll break your heart." I heeded him and never have.

Laird, Sal, Anne, Rob

8 SUMMER SIBLINGS—SUMMER CAMPS

Because I was so much younger than my siblings, I got to know them mainly during the summers. When I think of them, I immediately think of the times that we sang together, especially on summer nights when we washed dishes and harmonized over the sound of running water and plates being scraped. At these times—even though I was four years younger than Rob, I was a totally accepted part of the clan—probably because I was the group soprano. When not singing, I was mostly considered a brat and too young to bother with, except by Sal, who treated me like the sister I was. When I think of my siblings I think first of her, and feel warm inside.

Sal, was known for her good humor, practicality and notable athletic abilities—witness her Angel Gabriel on Christmas Eve. Even if you'd just been introduced to her at a party, she would draw you into the conversation and you'd feel comfortable with her. Her hair was straight and sandy colored. Here clothes were down-to-earth: plain white blouses, hardy tweed skirts and saddle shoes. She took me out on the barn floor and taught me how to dance, play ping pong, and hit middle C on the old piano in the corner. She taught me how to play tennis, swim, behave with boys and do hundreds of other things. She was strong in all ways and never critical.

One time, she used her unusual strength to help me out of a bad situation. During the summer we rented in Nantucket, Sal her husband, Ernie, took me out in their car to teach me how to drive. It was in the afternoon and suddenly we were hit by a thunderstorm and a downpour. Ernie said "Drive home, but not too fast!" and as we wove our way through the Nantucket streets up to our house, the rain got worse, and then even worse. Our neighbor's house was smack next to ours and, by mistake, I drove into their driveway and because of the heavy rain the dirt driveway was so slippery that when I put on the brake, we skidded into the garage door and cracked two of its boards. At this point, we sank into the driveway's mud and were stuck. We all got out of the car and Ernie and Sal squeezed themselves in front of the car, and with a "let's go," they shoved and shoved the car back out into the street. If Sal had been a small woman without muscles, this couldn't have happened. Then Ernie rushed into our house, found nails and a hammer and fixed the broken slats. The neighbors never knew, and later on, due to Ernie's training, I got my license. Sal had been there, again, to help me out of trouble.

Sal may have been strong but, when young, she sported the worst buck teeth ever—a mold of them is in the Washington Dental School. Her teeth were so bad that Mother and Dad had no choice but to spend a ton of money on having our dentist straighten them out. The day this was done, Sal sneaked home, picked me up and took me uptown to the Five and Dime store. We went to the toy department and to Sal's extreme delight, found a pair of wax buck teeth. We then went home. Sal told me to hide in the bushes and then rang the doorbell. Mother opened the door and Sal, with her buck teeth sticking out of her mouth gurgled, "Mutha—sumpfin tewabul haff happened to my teeeff!" Mother's face went white with shock until Sal pulled out the false teeth. Mother burst out laughing but, then said, "Sal, this isn't funny!"

Sal and I spent one summer at the Four Winds camp in Maine where it turned out that she was the youngest counselor, and I was the oldest camper. I was always being called "Madam" by my fellow campers and her fellow counselors called her "kid." So, one day, she made diapers for herself out of a bath towel and a cane for me and we spent the day acting our designated ages. Sal knew that if we made fun of ourselves, others would stop making fun of us. It worked.

Sadly, Sal died too young from cancer. She was an outstanding mother and, to me and her kids, she is still alive. We talk to her often.

Sister on Her Way

We have an old grainy movie of her,
cartwheeling across the lawn
in front of our New Hampshire barn,
cartwheeling toward the road.

There she goes,
her arms, her legs, gyroscopic,
spinning, spinning,
her body filled with gym and vigor,
her kid's face daring us,
grinning.

Whee!
Look at me!
I'm on my way!
Please!
Let me please you
with my play!

On holidays when we were young
she stayed with me
when I was frightened by the night.
She listened to my fears,
cuddled, held me tight.

Years later, she hurt her back.
I played nurse and cuddled her,
as I do now,
as she goes spinning, spinning,
toward another road, another sphere,
where all her giving, kindness, bravery,
will hold her,
safe.
Where heavenly arms—
Will hold her dear.

Anne was the glamorous one. She had high cheekbones, a slightly rounded nose and short, snappy, brownish hair. I loved her long, absolutely gorgeous, "gams"—the ones, that when crossed, perked up Sunday church. She was a graceful, strong, swimmer, but not seriously into athletics. Anne would rather talk, smoke, make people laugh, and, like Mother, organize. I never remember her not dressed in the latest styles looking—what we'd later call, "hip." Early on, the word "funny" described my relationship with Anne. We had "lots and lots of pun" together, wrote funny songs for friends' birthdays and family affairs and spent hours on the phone keeping in touch. But, sadly, this closeness didn't last.

When I was in my late forties and Reid and I had moved up to the Berkshires in western Massachusetts, Anne and I had a critical falling out, caused by a silly joke. Anne was on an ocean cruise with her husband, Harry, and sent me a picture of a fellow traveler who was as blonde as I was, and rather fat. On the back of the snapshot she'd written "Looks just like you!" I was blond, yes, but not at all fat so I sent her a postcard which said, "Either you need new glasses or I need to go on a major diet!" There was a smiling face at the bottom of my note. A few days later I received what I've always referred to as "the blue letter," a three-page, handwritten letter on blue stationary. According to Anne's letter, I would never have any friends in my life and wherever I lived I would live without love! Anne's "WMD"—Words of My Destruction—was the product of *her* mass destruction caused by martinis. I tried to communicate with her, but with no luck. Even when I had (an easily removed) bit of breast cancer, she never called. I called and called her, but she was always, "too busy to talk." After years of this, there came a day when President George W. Bush made a hysterical blunder during an interview. Knowing how Anne felt about Bush, I called her and, before she could say anything, I imitated Bush and she burst into laughter—our silence was broken. We never discussed the Blue Letter. It no longer mattered—we were friends again.

There is one time with Anne I won't forget. It was during our good days. Anne was around nineteen years old and I was ten. This night there had been a party in the barn and Anne, having snuck too many drinks, was tipsy, thereby more open to showing her inner feelings. We'd finished our post-party supper in the kitchen and it being a hot night, we walked out to the front lawn next to the dirt road. The night was spectacularly clear and filled with a massive web of stars. Anne waved her arms up to the skies and suddenly fell down, laughing. I lay down beside her and looked up at the beauty above. Suddenly, she stopped laughing and, pointing to the sky, said, "God, I hate that! I really hate that!!"

"Hate what?" I asked.

"I'm terrified of that Nothing up there" she replied. "That dark and all that space."

I pointed to the sky and said, "That nothing is filled with stars and a moon and probably more than we will ever know."

She put her hands over her eyes and said, "that's what I'm afraid of—not knowing."

Sisters in Space

Remember how you could not face
those star-struck August nights
for fear of "all that space"?
Instead, you knuckled out the fright of stars;
turned your head into the grass,
toughing out the fiery fling
spinning toward the two of us
spread-eagle on the lawn—
like finger-food
beneath a ravenous moon.

For you,
the fact of endless roads of black
between the burning stars
was more than mind could bear.
You saw yourself in spin,
forever turning toward no end—
no basement door,
no picture frame,
no period to the sentence,
no chiming noon ...
just tumbling there,
sucked dry to ash.
Safer to inhale a Lucky Strike,
a drink,
and laughing, -
make me harmonize, again,
"Oh, Mr. Moon."

Remember?
We were nuclear then.
Fissioned out of common cell.
Blasted into carousels of unreined summers,
flying blind,
doubled over,
splitting a gut,
cracking up ...
handling high hilarity like TNT
until our own Enola Gay
bombayed us out and down,
leaving nothing but irradiated rubble,
and maimed,
we were done...

except for when I bend back to a summer night
and recognize our shadows
in the black between the stars.
Can't you see? We could be there,
romping,
but for lack of sun.

Anne, like Sal, died too early in her life. She had suffered
the too early loss of her wonderful husband, Harry, who,
tragically, had died from his allergy to peanuts, and this had
contributed to her genetically based overuse of alcohol.
Even though she'd become a member of AA, she still died
from excessive smoking and her many years of drinking,
but when I think of her now, I remember the day of her son
Henry's wedding. After the reception when all the guests
had left, Anne drove back home. As she got into the car I
said, "Anne, I love you." She rolled down the window and
said, "I love you, *too!*"—she hadn't said that in many,
many years. Now, when I think of her, I remember
moments like that; all the sister fun we had, and her
gorgeous Lauren Bacall legs streamlining through the water
on Silver Lake.

Rob, The Son, was the main actor during our teen years.
He played lacrosse and rode horses and every summer was

a star on the tennis court. He had Mother's blond, curly hair and high cheekbones and when he became a New Hampshire State Senator, he definitely looked the part.

An example of Rob's exalted family position occurred when I was a sophomore boarding at the elite Masters School, known as "Dobbs," in Dobbs Ferry, New York, and Rob was a sophomore at Princeton. As smoking was as normal in my family as eating, I took up the habit in my teens. Naturally, smoking at school was forbidden, but that didn't prevent students from puffing it up in secret places, like the woods by the school tennis courts.

Unsurprisingly, I was caught and, as a punishment, made to plant tulips in our headmistress's garden. Mother was furious—"shamed"—by my behavior. That same year, Rob—on a beer spree with some college buddies—was caught dancing down the Princeton Commons tables where students ate and was suspended for two weeks. My parents' reaction to this? They were upset, of course, but mostly they laughed. Dancing down the dining tables? Isn't this something any boy would do? Wasn't it *really* funny!

In the early years Rob considered me a brat and nothing else. The most familiar words I heard from him were, "Grow up!" and "You don't know *anything*." "Do you want to play?" was not a sentence I heard often. However, there were those fun nights of singing and because I sang high soprano, Rob considered me worthy. Rob was not happy when I married Reid—not a Princetonian but a Yalie! However, he was sarcastically cheery at our wedding. "Well, if you had to marry a "bulldog", I guess you did pretty well." He and I always connected through our humor, and when I was in college, he thought me cute enough to send me on a date with one of his college friends. This friend immediately came on to me and I was scared. I'd known passionate kisses and a bit more, but I'd never had a tall, muscular guy lunge at me, obviously with *a lot* in mind. I kept shouting, "Rob won't like this. He'll kick your butt!" He then backed off. When Rob heard about this, he reamed out his college buddy and was as horrified as a brother should be. Despite our typical brother-sister conflicts, Rob was a protective Batman to my Robin. Like Anne and Sal, Rob died too early and as with Anne and Sal, I remembered him with a poem:

Way More Than This

After the service
I sidled through your mourners by the church
to walk to my motel,
needing a moment of quiet
away from sad faces, words of loss.

You - athletic brother -
smart, busy, bossy,
blessed with humorous mind and song,
suddenly, tragically, too early,
you were gone.

I thought I was headed toward the reception,
but dazed by death,
I was turned around,
walking the wrong way,
walking toward town.

And, there you were,
borne by living arms,
boxed in as you'd never been before -
now "gray matter" of a different kind,
or, as you would say,
"asses to ashes, bust to dust".

Yes. There you were
soon to be bedded under stone,
one boasting your name, your dates,
no jokes, just facts alone.

154

Suddenly, I heard you say,
"Wait! There's more, - way, way more!".
There was. There is. There will be.
And knowing you –
you're on the phone,
making plans for a different day.

We did not spend every summer in New Hampshire—often
we were shunted away to summer camps or a rental house.
When I was about nine, Mother decided it was my time to
go to camp. Rob went to Camp Marienfeld in Chesham,
down the road from Green Pastures. Anne and Sally had
gone to the nearby Hill Camp for girls, which was situated
on our beloved Silver Lake, and later I was forced to do the
same. Being so much younger than Sal and Anne, I had the
questionable privilege of going to camp alone. Hill Camp
was run by a very strict woman and her daughter, the riding
teacher. We slept in small cottages in small double-decker
beds, and if anyone talked after bedtime, that person was
made to go outside in the dark and stand at attention for ten
minutes, with moths and mosquitos everywhere, until let
back in. Needless to say, we never spoke a word after our
camp counselor turned off the light.

"Mrs. B," the camp's owner and Queen of Discipline,
had an interesting, effective way of dealing with camp kids

who fought with each other. She would make them come into the main house's largest room and fit them out with boxing gloves. The rest of us were made to stand in a large circle around them. Then she'd count down from twenty and order the boxers to scream insults while circling and jabbing at each other. As we all watched the two girls fight, we'd shout encouraging words like, "Hang in there!" and "Good punch," all the while amazed at this form of punishment. Before long, as intended, the two enemies would begin laughing at the craziness of this ordered fight and, inevitably, would end up in hysterics, hugging each other. From then on, having shared this crazy experience, they were good friends.

Mrs. B's daughter was not as wise as her mother. She forced riding on everyone even if they were as terrified as I. Every morning we were taken down to the stables, placed on a horse and made to ride around a circular run, showing what we had learned the day before. I could trot, but my sweating hands were always so tight on the reins that the poor horse's neck could hardly lower, and she would rebuke me in front of the others. I became known by the other campers as the "Sissy Rider."

One day, we were taken out to ride down the dirt road that ran from the camp all the way to the dirt road that went by Green Pastures. On this particular day, my horse trotted off the road into the field to feed. I tried pulling his head up with the reins but he didn't want to stop eating, so I started jerking. It didn't work. Then, I pulled on my left rein to steer him away from his feeding ground and he took off so fast that I immediately pulled hard to the right. He rose up on his back legs; I fell to the ground; he stumbled back; rolled to the right and crumbled down by my legs. Luckily it was only the side of his head that hit me but it was enough to give me bruises for a few days. "Mrs. B's" daughter insisted I continue with the riding classes but every time I'd get on a horse, I'd tense up and sweat so much that riding was almost impossible. That was it. My teacher finally gave up and only made me brush the horses.

I hated this camp and was so homesick that I decided to run away. So, very early one morning, I snuck out of my cabin and worked my way down past the stables and started to climb the first hill on my long journey. Suddenly, I heard the roar of a vehicle behind me. When it got to me, it slowed and the man behind the wheel of a logging truck shouted through the window, "Are you lost?" I told the driver I was on my way home and told him where it was. He said, "Hop in," and off we went. He was a very nice man and took me all the way to our house. Mother and Dad then discussed the fact that I'd dared such a long walk from my hated camp—I didn't tell them about accepting a ride from a stranger— and, as it was near the end of summer, they let me stay.

A better camp story has to do with the notably liberal, hands-on Putney School Work Camp in Putney, Vermont. I went there when I was twelve and because you were allowed to think on your own and do adult work, such as building walks and repairing barns, I loved it. More than anything, I loved it because it was coed!

My roommate, Rachel Cohen, was from the Bronx. Despite our different backgrounds, we became close friends. We would go to the infirmary and sing and dance to cheer up the campers who'd sprained an ankle or had a summer cold and we'd shoot our toothbrushes at a dart board in our room. Most importantly, we shared stories and childhood angers, something I'd never dared do before. When I returned home, I told Mother I wanted to have Rachel come visit. Mother said," I don't think she'd feel comfortable, Laird." This was my first knowledge of snobbism and prejudice, two diseases of the times. Sadly, I never saw Rachel again.

One of my favorite memories of Putney Camp, is of Barney, a short and thin boy from the Bronx with a long nose and big wide eyes. He was the youngest camper and, in my mind, the weirdest one there. He would stand outside and for a quarter, he would—yuck—swallow a live worm. He would slurp it into his mouth and holding his nose, gulp it down. He made quite a bit of money that summer.

Amazing to me, I was voted that summer's Best Camper and given a special badge and a letter of praise from the headmaster of the Putney School. He talked to me about the possibility of my attending Putney. I was thrilled, as I was at the age when choice of a boarding school was top of my parents' list. I came home, told them I really wanted to go to this school next year. The headmaster had even written them a letter saying he hoped I would attend the school. I begged, but again, Mother, the cultural critic, didn't like my choice. "Too many communists there" Sadly, Daddy succumbed to her opinion and I was made to go to another boarding school where commies were not to be found. However, hysterically funny times were found and during the last years of boarding school, the great, inherited fun of holding a martini glass in my hand became a school course for which I got very good marks.

Olive Oiled

9 STRAIGHT UP OR ON THE ROCKS?

Undoubtedly, by now, you've come to realize there was a fair amount of drinking in my family. Fair? How about way-too-much! Perhaps Father T's recipe for "bathtub gin" was reborn in our genes, as most of us caught the disease.

Not surprisingly, one of the first sounds I remember was the shucka shucka sound of Daddy shaking up martinis outside on the small grass terrace of Green Pastures. At six o'clock, after a tennis game and shower, the players, smelling of Ivory Soap, would assemble to have drinks on the entryway to our house. Sitting in mother's perfect "country chairs," or on the low stone wall flanked by her tiger lilies, they would drink their cocktails while they ate cheese and crackers; smoked Camels; joked about their tennis shots and, inevitably, we kids and Dad would sing one of his funny old songs.

The main characters of the post-tennis martini crowd were Bill Eustis, Daddy and Mother; Sal, Rob, and Anne and usually houseguests. Except for myself, none of this group drank ginger ale or cider. I would look at the crowd, worshipping them, wishing that I, too, could have some of that "juice" in a pretty glass, especially that one with the pretty green thing in it. In the distance we could see all of beautiful Mount Monadnock. It was perfectly shaped and on most martini nights the evening sun highlighted its peak. As I'd watch the laughing crowd, my eyes moving from them to the distant mountain, the sound of another shaker being tossed would inevitably bring me back to the happy drinkers, all of them with glass in hand. Except for Sal. Her gin and tonic was usually untouched, sitting by her side on the grass; her eyes fixed on the mountain—a smile on her face.

When he was seventy-one, Rob died of an embolism and

if he'd not been a heavy drinker, might have recovered. Anne lived until she was eighty, but most of her last years were spent suffering from the effects of smoking and drinking. Dad and mother, both alcoholics, died—still drinking and puffing away. Sal, the only one of us with eyes wide open to the beautiful, clear mountain beyond, survived longer than any of them and although she finally died of cancer, she died with a glass of clear water by her bed.

In my youth I thought of drinking as a part of our "funny" times—and it was. Growing up, I began to see that a highball, always somewhere near my parents was like another member of the family. In the summers, when we were at Green Pastures and Dad was not working, he and Mother would sip on martinis as the sun went down. No wine at dinner but afterward there was bourbon while Mother knitted on her chaise and Dad read to us. These times, when we got to sit with them and sip our ginger ale were, unfortunately, over shadowed by those later times when I'd find Mother crying upstairs or stomping down the hall, full of anger and booze. Thankfully, though, when I was young, most of the drinking accompanied funny times.

One summer morning, when I was ten and Anne nineteen, I wanted to take a sunbath and Anne whispered,

"Come with me!" Dressed in shorts and a shirt over her bathing suit and carrying a big handbag, she led me across the roof of the colonnade between our rectory and the church, which ended just underneath the roof of the church chapel. She'd brought two beach towels and we climbed the little ladder to the roof, sat down, and started slathering ourselves with baby oil and iodine to get a quick tan. Then, from her big bag, she pulled out a bottle of vodka, a bag of ice, and a paper cup, and while she sat there sipping away, we talked about the graveyard below and how she'd plan to meet her boyfriend some night to do some necking. Nobody would look in a graveyard for neckers would they? I loved hearing about this and so we started talking about boys. She gave me advice on how to get them to like me, how to wear my hair, and other helpful hints such as what clothes looked good and how to handle Mother's moods. I was too young to think anything of the fact that Anne was drinking so early in the morning and on the roof of a church no less. I didn't see it as the foreboding sign of what was to come later in her life.

The first time I tasted liquor, I was about to enter my senior year at boarding school and, during one cocktail hour, Dad came to me, handed me a glass of sherry and said, "You may be offered a drink by some boy at a party so you better know what it tastes like and that you have to be careful of how much you drink,"— this coming from a heavy drinker. I didn't like the taste, but, sure enough, during that year I had my first drink and I learned to like it – after all, wasn't it something my whole family did, something normal? No. it wasn't, as I found out early on.

Despite my thinking that drinking was another word for "fun" there was one summer when I found out the danger it could bring. I was in boarding school and I went to visit my close friend, Joanie Barber, whose parents had a house in chic, rich East Hampton, Long Island. Joanie and I would often hang out at the snazzy Maidstone Club to swim and meet boys. One day a boy named Tim offered to take me home in his fancy Mercedes. When we started to drive, he was weaving all over the road. I knew he was drunk and I knew I had to get out fast but also knew that if I asked him to stop, he probably wouldn't. So, instead, I started groaning as if in pain and looking down at my legs.

"What's the matter?" he asked.

"Oh shit", I said." I just got my period and I'm bleeding like mad. I gotta get out. Please! Stop!"

Not wanting blood all over his expensive leather seats, he stopped and I leapt out and quickly ran away, afraid when he started up he might hit me with his car. When Tim came after me I told him I wasn't getting back into the car. He took off at a furious speed and I was soon picked up by a passerby who drove me home. Not too many years later, despite interventions from friends, Tim died from his excessive drinking.

Fun and drinking seemed perfectly fine to me and I had no idea of how it could affect my behavior. When I was a senior at boarding school I started dating Peter, a boy I met through Sal and her husband, Ernie, and later became engaged to. One weekend, he invited me to his home in Greenwich, Connecticut. I knew little about Greenwich, so had no idea how posh it was and what I was in for. As we drove down Peter's street, I could see royal estates back in the woods. Wow! Finally, we slowed down in front of a nice small house and I commented on what a pretty house he lived in. Peter turned into the driveway and casually said, "Oh, that's our gatehouse." He then sped up and drove what seemed like miles up his driveway to finally park in front of a colonial Buckingham Palace. A uniformed maid immediately emerged from the mansion. She took our bags and I followed her upstairs to my elegant room, where I changed into something more presentable and went down to meet his parents for cocktails. After two stiff martinis and lots of small talk, we went to the dining room; a room so large and impressive it could have housed the Queen Mother and her entourage. Wine was on the table in crystal decanters. Silver forks and knives hugged the sides of small Limoges china plates and sitting on top of them were delicate glass fingerbowls. The bowls were half filled with water and floating on top were fragile little rose petals, far more appealing than Mother's usual grapefruit halves sitting on a glass plate.

Mother had taught us proper dining behaviors, but this table was as long as an airport runway and there were only four of us, so far from each other that yelling might be necessary. I was so nervous that all I could do was stare straight down at my fingerbowl. Peter's parents were talking, but their voices seemed miles away. I had been to large dinner parties, but there always had been people clustered at the table—people I knew. This dinner was terrifying. All I could see was my fingerbowl with the rose petals floating on top. Suddenly, I heard a voice saying, "A rose in a glass is a soggy wet mass." I raised my head and looked around the table to see who in hell had made this outrageous remark. Everyone was staring at me. To my horror I realized those outrageous words had come out of *my* mouth without my permission. I bent my head again.

That's when I heard laughter. Peter's parents were in hysterics. They thought what I'd said so amusing that, apparently, at later dinner parties, they quoted me every time they used the fingerbowls. Once more, drinking had produced big laughs, but as the years went on, it didn't.

The first time we had actual evidence that our Mother had a serious problem was when Anne went into Mother's room to steal a squirt of perfume. She came out reeking of gin—she'd tapped Mother's secret stash and it was now behind her ear. Dad was not a serious drinker during his months of work, but during the summers, and as he aged, his drinking got worse. A few years before my parents died, Sally sent them a letter, signed by all of us, saying that we were all worried about their drinking. Daddy responded thanking us for our "concern," but that they were "fine." Long ago I found a letter Dad wrote Mother when, unbeknownst to us, she was at Silver Hill, an elegant rehab center. A doctor had recommended this place for learning to "control her drinking." Dad wrote her saying that he was very proud of her. "I'm not drinking", he said, "except for when I'm with friends, or if I'm having trouble sleeping. Then, I only have a small brandy after dinner." "Not drinking"?...Oh, sure.

It is sadly ironic that Dad never went to AA, where he

would have come face to face with the two main subjects of his sermons—a higher power and the fellowship of man. Even having grown up a minister's daughter with the church playing a major part in my life, I never fully understood or experienced God's higher power and the true meaning of the fellowship of man. Yes, I prayed to him (her? It?), but those prayers were mostly calling God to step in and fix something. If my prayers weren't answered (and they rarely were), I just figured he hadn't picked up his phone—or he didn't exist.

Later in my life, drinking became my liquid God as it washed away those childhood scars and my fears of life's barn bats, but then it became an ocean that almost washed me away ... until fate walked in. One day, sober but suffering a nasty hangover, I slipped on a bathroom rug, fractured my elbow in three places and had two operations that led to three months of rehab in a hospital. Needless to say, the doctors and nurses didn't offer cocktails, so when I came home I had met sobriety, but now needed to learn its language. A friend immediately took me to AA and my travels began. It was the first time that I'd sat down with a group of people I didn't know and found myself talking about personal subjects. But soon I realized we spoke the same language and came from the same town—Cocktail

Corners. They all seemed very interested in something called a "higher power,"— another word for God.

At the beginning of my AA travels I didn't buy the higher power thing, but over time it became a regular visitor in my life and finally, it moved in to live with me. (When I came home from my months of rehab, my famously unfriendly cat crawled up beside me and started doing what cats are supposed to do—purr. From then on I called her "my higher purrer.")

Even though I no longer drink, I still can summon up humor when surrounded by drinkers. Last year I went to a large, sit down Thanksgiving party. I was seated next to a man I'd never met and, as always, wanting to get a laugh, when the turkey was presented at the table, I said, "Oh goodie, I'll just GOBBLE, GOBBLE it up." My dinner partner turned to me and with no expression on his face said, "I have NO sense of humor!" – That was almost the end of my humor ...but not quite.

As the wines were passed and passed everyone was getting tiddly, including the humorless man by my side who was drinking and drinking like an old cat on a hot day. When a new wine was poured, he'd lift his glass, hold it under his nose and say. "ahhhhh, an '82". Next time around he'd do the same thing, saying "Ahhh, a '95." So tired of this crap, I raised my cranberry juice, dramatically sniffed it and said, "Ahhh, un cranneberge... 2015". Most of the guests knew I drank cranberry juice and howled with laughter. But not my dinner partner.

I am a new person now. I am able to talk with some dinner party asshole and dig down enough to often find a basically nice person underneath the annoying façade. I am able to look at myself with a clearer eye and now realize that this "higher power" is out there—or within— to be drawn on to help handle life's problems. I have told people that the best thing that ever happened to me was being an alcoholic—and it is. It has given me a new life.

Judy and Laird: Sun of a beach!

10 SCHOOLS, INK-ORPORATED.

Summers at Green Pastures were like a never-never land, but when September arrived, the reality of school enveloped me with its onslaught of challenges, not all of them academic.

After I graduated from the Peck School in Morristown, I started my first year at boarding school. My parents were only able to afford this elite school because Dad knew the headmistress, known for her kindness and approachability, and thanks to her I received a minister's scholarship. Unfortunately, she left the year I started. She was replaced by a new headmistress and assistant headmistress, who four years later—the year I graduated—were dismissed for "bad behavior," which included drinking, mishandling of funds and lesbianism—a no-no in those days. They should have added mistreatment of students as they were superb at that. I'll never forget the day I arrived at school and met Samantha, my roommate. When I came through the door she rushed to greet me, shook my hand so hard that it almost dropped off and said in a low voice, "Hi. My name is Samantha– just call me Sam!" She had very short brown hair, wore a man's shirt, a man's tweed jacket, Argyll socks, and sneakers. Without chatting, she began taking tightly folded men's shirts out of her suitcase and slinging them into her open bureau drawers with the accuracy of a professional Frisbee player.

Sam had been living in Massachusetts with her grandparents since her parents had been killed in a car accident. Athletics, her natural talent, kept her busy and happy and she was very nice, but we had little in common except one thing—we hated our headmistresses.

My first introduction to Miss D, the new headmistress, was on a Sunday night at the compulsory all-student

"Reflection Meeting" in the school auditorium. These meetings were ones where Miss D. would preach about student behavior. All of us would sit with our mouths theatrically agape, as if stunned by what was being said. Sometimes, we actually were. Miss D's lectures relayed the message that behaving like a typical teenager was not allowed in her school. Yes, we could play, but only at "play time"; we were not to walk hand in hand with any visiting boys; there would be "room checks." Sam and I soon learned a trick to transform the lectures. We would pucker up our lips and, like a teakettle heating up, hiss very, very softly. Soon, others were doing it as well. It was so low a hiss that it sounded like something had gone wrong with the heating system. Miss D., curious about the sound, would stop her preaching to check on the radiators. We would sit back, stifling giggles.

Another ruse was for one of us to suddenly start sobbing as if in deep emotional pain. This, of course, brought attention, followed by comforting actions from the other students. Inevitably, this ended with Miss D having to suggest the student be taken to her room. Both of these tricks provided a way to shorten the damn Sunday evening lecture.

We also had discovered a method of surviving the times

when Miss D. would bring us to her office for a one-on-one scolding. She would make us sit across from her while she lectured and gave threats of study hall for a week. We learned to look—not into her eyes—but just above her eyebrows, which forced her to crane her head up and then sweep it around and around, trying to make eye contact. It got so that we didn't dread the threats of study hall punishment as eye-revenge was worth it.

Miss D. and her assistant, Miss L., practiced personal habits that included excessive drinking and their supposedly secret personal relationship. When I became a senior, I had good enough marks to be allowed to live in the school's palatial building called Estherwood, a nineteenth-century palace that also housed the headmistresses. I had four roommates and our room was directly over the headmistresses' huge bedrooms. There was a long, royal, circular staircase that led from their floor up to ours. At night, we would hear the two of them having drunken fights below. Our bedroom floor would shake as they stomped around their room, and there was nothing left to do but wait it out, until they collapsed into their beds. Eventually, we came up with a way to survive their fights. Wearing our shoes, we would stand on our beds and then leap off, making so much noise that our beds would rock.

Then we'd wait to hear the pounding of feet racing up the circular staircase. Miss D. would throw open our door and shout, "What...is... going... on?" By that time, we'd be back in our beds, heads nestled on our pillows, eyes closed, feigning sleep. Then, seemingly startled awake, we'd snort and say, "Whaa? Whaa." Miss D. would look at us, and confused, teeter back downstairs.

Miss D and Miss L's "secret" relationship was ironic given that sexual behavior was a taboo subject at school. We were instructed not to talk about sex, or God forbid, practice it in any form. Whenever a boy's prep school glee club came to give a concert, Miss D. would deploy what we called the "Bush Patrol." She would get into her long Buick sedan and with a side searchlight on, she'd patrol the campus checking out the woods near the tennis courts and all the driveway bushes for "neckers." Lucky for us, she regarded the deep muddy school basement as too foul a place for anyone, so these underground rooms were where we'd go. I was still dating Peter and one glee club weekend we walked around "the circle"—a central walkway that could be seen from all buildings—(Seniors were allowed to walk there with their dates, because they could be observed from the school window.) On this weekend, Peter and I stopped for a quick kiss and out rushed Miss D. to sternly tell us, "bad behavior is not allowed here. Save it for home!" If she'd been in the school basement the night before, she'd not have cared much about a quick kiss!

The most telling school experience, relating to Miss D., and my father as well, occurred during my freshman year. I'd written many poems for my English class that fall, but hadn't kept copies of them. Come December, I was called to Miss D.'s office and made to sit, facing her across her desk. Staring at me with a snide smile on her face, she lifted a piece of paper from her desktop and said, "Laird— Miss Barkely has brought this from your English class files with a question of how you wrote this. It's very good, Laird, but it suggests you may not have written it yourself. You know you're not allowed to use someone else's poems, don't you?" I told her I hadn't copied it, but she paid no attention and continued, saying, "So, Laird, I'm going to have to ask you to recite it for me and, if you can, we'll forget about this." I couldn't believe it. I knew what plagiarism meant and I would never have been stupid enough to have done this. Thank God for ego and good memory—I had enough of each to be able to recite my poem and, with a disappointed smile on her face, Miss D. let me go.

I called my parents and told them about this and Daddy

was so angry that he came up to school the next day, demanding to see Miss D. She defended Miss Barkely and herself by saying, "But you see, Reverend Trowbridge, it was a poem way beyond her age of insight! You should take that as an example of her talent." Daddy told me about this and when I asked him what he'd said to her, he replied, "I told her, 'Yes—it's an example of her talent, but more important, it's an example of your meanness.' " Miss D. did not even look at me in the halls for months. Despite Miss Barkely's overreaction to my poem, she was an excellent teacher and my love of words—especially poetry— stems from her English Literature classes.

Writing and singing were—and still are—two of my favorite occupations. Having grown up with a constantly singing family, I was good enough to get into the school's very reputable, jazz-based singing group that sang and also performed musical skits at school functions and, occasionally, at boys' school dances. We happily doo-wopped our way through our otherwise wholly academic life. I finished my years at school being the president of our glee club. Now, when I think of that time, I try to think of my music and English classes. Sadly, though, when I think of boarding school, Miss D. is the first one that comes to mind.

Laird sings!

The year I graduated, Miss D. and Miss L. were fired for their transgressions and Dobbs now had a new head mistress. At that time, a woman on the school board questioned me about Miss D. and Miss L. When she asked if certain happenings were true, I nodded yes. By simply nodding I was not required to go through the legal procedure of giving testimony. A nod was enough and it meant final retribution for me. Now, when I get on-line announcements about that school, I most often delete.

After boarding school, I attended Mount Holyoke College in South Hadley, Massachusetts. Before I enrolled, I went to the campus to be interviewed, fell in love with Holyoke's beautiful and welcoming entrance gate and said to my parents, "I want to go there!"

Despite my early experience with mummies at the Boston Natural History Museum, I'd always wanted to become an archeologist, but when I found I'd have to take two full years, bent over, learning tiny Sanskrit writings, I decided to major in English and philosophy. These subjects fascinated me, but having been the child who had buried her toys from winter to spring in her backyard, every summer, when I'm vacationing in Nantucket, I become the archeologist and plow through the sandy areas on the moors for buried Wampanoag arrowheads, hoping to find an Indian burial ground. To be in the presence of something or someone ancient, tells us fascinating stories and speaks to the continuity of life. To this day, I wish I'd become an archeologist.

Despite my love for buried mysteries, English Lit became very important to me and definitely led me to my love of poetry and my love of writing. Miss Kauffman was my senior year English teacher and I still have some of her instructive comments saved in a memory box. Many years later, when she was an elderly lady, I met her on a street in the Berkshires and we hugged and had a good laugh remembering our college days. Another memorable class was Music Harmony, with another professor, this one having no personality at all.

Music, especially playing the piano, had always been a treasured part of my life. At a young age, I was able to hear a tune on the radio and sit down at the piano and play it. I could only manage to make three-note chords, but the music was there—from ear to keyboard. I even wrote a three-part "symphony" which was played by our church's organist. My well-tuned ear benefited my singing, and at college, my best friend, Judy, and I were in a college singing group called the V-8's. Judy and I also had great fun being in college shows together. Because all I knew about music was basically learned through my ears, I decided that maybe I should learn the "rules" of music, so I took a class called Music Harmony. Judy took the same class.

Our teacher was very handsome, but had as much humor as a snail. His class was mathematical and boring, except for the fact that Judy was in the class with me. So bored with Professor Handsome's methods, we purposefully sat at opposite ends of the front row so that we wouldn't start laughing. However, we couldn't resist throwing some humor into our hour of boredom. So just before the class officially began, Judy would yell to me, "How's hominy?" I'd answer "Grit!" She'd reply, "Getting butter and butter!" Our teacher would stare across at us from his desk, while the rest of the class tittered. After three or four days of this, our professor told us that we weren't funny and to "shut up or leave." We shut up, but to this day we say our lines whenever we meet.

Judy and I both had boyfriends who went to nearby Amherst College. My boyfriend was Ridley, Judy's was Ned. On weekends, they'd pick us up in Ridley's car and drive us to Amherst College where we'd sing and drink it up as we made the rounds of frat houses. One winter weekend we were driving over the mountain between South Hadley and Amherst, when we hit a patch of ice and started skidding toward the outer edge of the road. Judy and I were sitting in the back seat but we could clearly see out the front window. The road's railing was only three feet high, and beyond it was a cliff that went straight down to nowhere. Terrified, my mind went into slow motion, seeing the railing slowly coming towards us. Suddenly, something flew through the air. It was Ridley—jumping into the backseat and landing on us. Meanwhile, in those seconds,

Ned was trying to brake slowly and steer the car away from disaster. Using their brains to surpass their fear, Ridley and Ned had instinctively known that more weight in the back of the car would slow it down—and it did. The sliding car finally stopped and we inched our way out, only to see that our car's nose was at the very edge of the steep precipice below. Judy and I voted our Ridley and Ned the smartest guys ever.

The town of Amherst was of great interest to me, not only because of my boyfriend, but because Emily Dickinson had lived there. Poetry had been my love since fourth grade so, naturally, I was more than eager to take the tour through her historic house on Main Street. Seeing the little table where she wrote and the rather gloomy rooms she lived in, made her poetry even more meaningful. To me, as to others, there seemed to be echoes of Emily's moods in every room. I was not alone in that feeling. Her poem, "One not need be a chamber to be haunted," has always had special meaning for me and came to the forefront a few years ago, when I had a strange experience.

One night, after I'd finished reading a biography about Emily's life, I turned out my light and went to sleep. I always keep a yellow writing pad on my bedside table, just in case I have an idea relating to my writing. That night my yellow pad was in its usual place. The next morning, I woke up and there was something, in my handwriting, scrawled on the pad and the pad, itself, was on the floor— not on the table. I had absolutely no memory of waking up during the night and I was stunned to see my writing on the pad:

My colors, all, have risen up—
Like bottom leaves in pond.
Yellow banners—signaling,
The warring fish below.

I have no time for hidden springs
To mulch me into ground,
But must float up and flag myself—
A dare to winter's blow.

I showed this poem to my writing coach and she pointed out that I'd never used dashes between words before (something Emily Dickinson was known for) and that the poem was not my usual style. Unfortunately, she did not say, "Oh, this is Emily Dickinson's work!" Still, I love to think that maybe I've inherited a small bit of Mother's ESP and that Emily was rough-drafting a poem to me. Because of this happening, a friend of mine gave me a rag doll of Emily in a white dress with her reddish hair pulled back in a bun. It sits by my desk, and I say "Hi" to her every day.

Right next to Emily is a picture of me on my graduation day from Mount Holyoke. My parents are at my side. Mother's eyes ask, "What do we do with her now?" The answer is that it's time for me to go home and get ready to go to work in the real world.

I'm gonna wash that boss right outa my hair

11 PIECES OF WORK

As women in the fifties were meant to cook, clean, be mothers and go to bridge clubs, I was unusual because I was not married, couldn't cook a boiled egg, and dared to get a job as—wow!...a secretary. Unlike other girls, I was going to be the secretary to an important, powerful boss, not just the nice guy who ran the florist shop down the street. It didn't matter that I ended up with important bosses, most of whom called me "doll"; what mattered was that I made dollars. It didn't matter that most of them were "pieces of work." I survived—often with a laugh. It all began in the town of Wynnewood, Pennsylvania.

The summer after graduation, I went to visit my friend, Judy, in Wynnewood, and stayed at her home for two weeks while I attended a nearby secretarial school. During this time, I learned how to type thirty-five words a minute and how to write "Dear Sir" and "Sincerely yours" in Gregg shorthand—a bit slow for someone who wanted to get a job. When the summer was over I went to an employment agency and interviewed at the Rockefeller Foundation. Because of a past connection between Father T. and John D. Rockefeller—and definitely not because of my typing skills—I got a job writing dull letters to benefactors. I didn't care—it meant money. However, after a few months, I couldn't take the boredom and decided it was time to quit.

During this time I had occasion to have tea with Dad's very rich cousin, Miss Susan Bliss, who lived in New York City. Cousin Sue had become our family's good friend and sometimes benefactor. She kindly helped supplement Dad's meager minister's salary, thus helping us all. She was our fairy godmother. When Anne was born she came down in her Packard limousine to my parent's tiny apartment in New York and helped with household chores. Despite her being brought up with a golden spoon in her mouth and a huge pile of cash on her highchair, she was not above washing dishes.

I had never been to Cousin Sue's home before. She lived at 9 East 68th Street and when I saw it, I realized it was a palace, not a "town house", as it was labeled. This palace, (now referred to as the Bliss Mansion) had been inspired by Palladian buildings in Vicenza, Italy. Cousin Sue had inherited this magnificent residence and, inside, were pieces of notable art works and antique furniture. Everything had some historic importance. She had never married but reputedly had been engaged to a French Count who broke off the engagement because his family didn't approve of him marrying a "commoner"—even a rich one. The truth was that Cousin Sue did not love this man and, unlike women of her time, refused to participate in an arranged marriage and so, courageously, broke off the engagement.

I'll never forget that afternoon tea. Cousin Sue and I sat on a lovely silk settee surrounded by artifacts. There was a sparkling chandelier hanging above and much of the furniture dated back to the eighteenth century. While chatting about college, I looked behind the settee at a Victorian table and commented on a small china and gold box with the letter *N* encrusted with diamonds on the top. "What is this beautiful little box?" I asked. "And what does the *N* stand for?" Cousin Sue leaned over to look and casually said, "Oh, yes—that's Napoleon's snuff box."

She was so off-handed she could have been talking about a box of Oreos. Then, looking at me with questioning eyes she asks, "Laird, have you ever been out west?" When I tell her "No" she asks "What have you planned for this summer?" I tell her that I have nothing planned except my usual time at Green Pastures. There's a pause and then she says, "How would you like to go out west to a ranch and, of course, take a friend?" I'm stunned. I'd never been anywhere that far away and this is an incredible offer. Plus—I could bring a friend! Maybe I'd finally learn to like riding horses.

Cousin Sue arranged the whole trip and I decided to take my good friend, Sandra Bramhall, whom I'd known since Peck School. We were going to the 3-Twenty Ranch outside of Bozeman, Montana, near the famous Madison River—known for its fly fishing and trout. Sandra and I boarded a train and, with our ranch clothes, traveled to Bozeman and the 3-Twenty. It was charming with cabins that looked out onto to a massive line of mountains. We had never seen anything like this before. It was set on a large, flat tract of land and the mountains were dramatically high, so different from our familiar New England surroundings. After registering, we were shown to a one-room wood cabin. It had a small porch attached by narrow columns to the roof above. The ranch's main building was not far away, but our cabin was out on an open plain.

When Sandra and I went to dinner in the main house, we were introduced to the other guests. One was the head seismologist at Montana State University. Another was Thomas Mendenhall, president of Smith College. Both were good-natured and funny so we were always assured of a good laugh at dinner. Our other new friends were Nick and Chuck who took care of the stables and the "old reliables— aka mustangs—not the uptight, trim, silky kind I'd known at Hill Camp or like the one who'd rolled on me. I remember being terrified when I took my first ride up to the nearby line of mountains. Chuck had my horse on a lead while he showed me the proper way to rock while trotting. "Just pretend you're boogying. It'll work." He was right. Both Chuck and Nick were like the cowboy actors Sandra and I had known in Western movies; tall, lanky and good looking, so we rode a lot. To this day I can remember the swinging waltz rhythm of riding Western saddle.

When not riding in the mountains, I started to learn about fly fishing. President Mendenhall decided I'd make a good ranch-advertisement, but only if I returned home knowing how to fish, so each day we'd meet at a cove by the Madison River and gear up. He was a patient teacher and I was soon gracefully arcing out my line and even pulling in some decent sized trout. I loved it and I began to do more fishing than riding.

One morning I went to fish by myself. About to climb down to the riverbank, I suddenly heard loud stomping and snorting sounds coming from below. There, getting ready to drink from the river, was a mother moose with her baby. Hearing me, their heads turned up and their eyes stared right into mine. I was a human being, an intruder, an alien to this part of their world. I'd been warned about the danger of meeting a mother and calf, so I knew this alien better get out of moose territory—fast!

I didn't dare run, for fear that they'd run after me, so I frantically tried to think of another way to escape. Then I saw a way out. A tall thin tree was nearby, but it only had branches high up. It didn't matter. It was a tree, a savior. So, using a strength I never knew I had, I shinnied up the tree and for a good hour, clung there with my legs wrapped around its trunk, hardly breathing, until—finally—the moose and her baby wandered off. That was the end of my solo fishing expeditions. It taught me an important lesson: if you have to shinny to save your life—do it!

My moose experience was frightening, but nothing in comparison to what happened on Aug 17, 1959, at 11:39 pm. For some reason, Sandra had gone home earlier than scheduled and so I now spent the nights alone in the tiny shack with only an oil lamp on my bedside table. That night I was snuggled up reading an Agatha Christie mystery in the cabin. Suddenly, I heard a low growling sound and to my amazement, the cabin began to slowly chug its way around in a circle. Obviously, a moose or elk had caught his antlers in the porch beams and was trying to get loose. Being smart enough to think of possible trouble, I blew out my lamp and then grabbed a flashlight to see what was happening on the porch. There was nothing happening on the porch, but there was plenty happening on the land all around. The moon was so bright that I could see all the way across the dirt plain to the ranch's main house and everywhere I looked, there were zigzagging lines cracking the earth and the sound of low, deep breathing in the background. I'd only seen an earthquake in movies, but this was the real thing. I quickly grabbed my cigarettes and flashlight, (both absolutely necessary), and ran, jumping over deep cracks, until I finally reached the main house where everyone has gathered. The Montana seismologist had rigged up a long rope with metal hooks hanging from it and, with the rope strung across the room, was carefully measuring the movement of the hooks, mumbling "A seven. seven and a half. Maybe more."

It turned out we'd had a 7.3 intensity earthquake and it had stranded a group of campers from another ranch by the Madison River. Luckily, they survived the night but two locals had drowned. Our road had dropped twenty-some feet. Nick and Chuck had lost two horses who'd run away. Needless to say, the summer was over.

At this time, I was still dating Ridley, my Amherst boyfriend, so after calling my parents with news of the earthquake, I called Ridley. I knew he was going to be driving to San Francisco in his old MG convertible to look for a job. I didn't look forward to another boring New York job, plus I wanted to be with him and what could be more fun than being with him in a MG? My Long Island friend, Joanie, had a sister in San Francisco and I could call her and maybe stay for a few days? Maybe Ridley and I could both get jobs? I could type thirty-five words a minute, couldn't I? I was now actually able to write most of a letter in shorthand. So, why not go to San Francisco? Oh God—I don't have anything to wear but jeans and boots. Oh well, I'll figure it out..

Joanie's sister, Sue, lived right in the city and when I called to ask if I could borrow some clothes she said, "No problem. You can stay with us and as for clothes—I'm pregnant, so you can borrow my normal ones while you look for work." My parents were surprised by the news of my heading out west, but I lied, telling them I was just going out for a short visit and was being driven by a friend I'd met at the ranch. Instead, I went with Ridley in his snazzy MG convertible.

Riding with "Roadster-Ridley"

On reaching San Francisco, I began a short stay with Sue, during which time I went to an employment agency, made friends with the agent and was sent for a slew of interviews. Sue hooked me up with a wonderful girl, Cynthia Kayan, who wanted to meet me. During our phone conversation, Cynthia asked what I looked like, (in case we met) and who I was. I didn't quite know how to answer, so I said, "I have two eyes, a nose, a mouth, blonde hair and I'm a girl." Luckily, Cynthia found this funny enough for her tastes and soon after meeting we became apartment mates.

After two weeks of searching, I landed a job with EOI (Executive Offices Incorporated), a decorating business for hotshot bosses. We made CEOs' offices glisten with the shine of money and, although my bosses were conservative business men, they were nice and with senses of humor.

Whenever the office phone rang I'd answer with the proscribed, "Hello, EOI." Cynthia, who was working at the Institute of International Education would answer, "Hello. IIE." So, whenever we called each other, I'd say "EOI"; she would say "IIE." Then, in unison, we'd sing "E,I,E,I,O" and roar with laughter, and, most of the time, our bosses joined in.

Our rental apartment was on Kearny Street below Coit

Tower, just off the Filbert Steps of Telegraph Hill, which inspired Jack Lemon's hit film, *"Under The Yum Yum Tree."* This was the beginning of some memorable times. The apartment was owned by a man named Jeff and his wife, Jane. Jeff was the spitting image of the handsome actor, Gig Young and, as he really liked young girls, he became a very helpful landlord. It was a small apartment but the back windows looked out to a house belonging to a famous bad-boy actor. I spent a lot of time looking outside trying to spot him. This made the apartment seem much bigger. The front windows faced the steep road that ended at the bottom of the Filbert Steps where all the tourists started out their final trek up to Coit Tower. I remember Kearny Street very well. One night, I had to grab my coffee pot and beat one of my dates out onto the street for being at bit too enthusiastic over my body. Sexy Jeff heard the loud noise and came to my rescue. Jeff was a regular visitor who came over for any reason, but he was helpful as he knew everything that was going on in the city and where to go for fun. One day I find out he has some other interesting connections.

On this day I come home from work and find my phone flashing a message. I call the number and immediately I hear a woman's voice asking if Jeff is there. I tell her she's called the apartment next to his, to which she replies, "Just tell him to call Maude regarding his hair appointment." I know where Jeff gets his hair cut, and that there are no women working there. I give the message to Jeff and he says, "Oh, that number was for me to call and find out when my nephew can get his hair cut." Now suspicious, I become a CIA agent and check the telephone book's number for Jeff's barber. It isn't the same number "Maude" has given me. Something strange is going on. Later, I tell a local gossip about this and she says "Oh, didn't you know? Jeff doesn't get haircuts, he gets "whore cuts!" He's a middleman in a ... ummm ... dating service." Good old Jeff—always open to new ideas.

Flash forward two years to 1960 when Cynthia and I moved back east to Manhattan. Because I needed money, I moved in with my parents who still lived in the famous, Dakota apartments. At this time Dad had his last job as Chaplain at St. Luke's Hospital. He could only afford the apartment as he'd been given a minister's discount. Living in the Dakota suited Mother to no end. The apartment was huge and perfect for her decorating talents. More importantly, she was—ta da—in the same building as Boris Karloff, Judy Holiday, and Lauren Bacall. When I'd leave each morning to go job hunting, Mr. Karloff would wave at me as he walked his dog down the block. He would tip his hat and smile and Dr. Frankenstein—his cinema-self—would disappear. Judy Holliday lived above our apartment and her son continuously rode his bike thunderously over our living room. Despite our love for her, we finally had to complain.

During that year, Ridley came back to Manhattan and one day I asked him over to see the elegant "joint." He wandered around and ended his tour in the kitchen. I was in the living room when I suddenly heard him shouting, "Wow! I *really* like this place!" He was standing at the kitchen window looking across the courtyard which faced Lauren Bacall's kitchen window. There she was, naked from the waist up, tossing lettuce at her sink—boobs bouncing in double-time. Ridley was in heaven.

And then came a red-letter evening when I went to a dinner party arranged by a friend of my parents. Both my parents and their friend knew a woman whose son they wanted me to meet. Anticipating I wouldn't have a good time with someone connected to my parents, I went, expecting the worst—and I got it. The young man's name was Reid White—the same boy I'd never met in Nantucket. He looked like Paul Newman, but he and I disagreed on almost everything and he was a Yalie, which, of course, meant he was an egotistic snob, but worse than that—he was going to vote for Kennedy! Because I happened to know two girls who... let's say... knew Kennedy very well, my opinion of him was not that of an admirable candidate and so I was going to vote for —good God— Nixon. This guy, Reid White, was aghast that Nixon was my choice, and we argued all evening. When it came time to leave, I went out to wave down a taxi. Reid offered to get one for me, but I let out a two-finger whistle and sped off in the cab without anything but a "goodnight." When I got back to the Dakota, I told my parents, "Well, I've met the great Reid White and you can have him!"

While at the Dakota, there came a night when, having had it with Mother and Dad's liquid behavior, I packed up and headed for the front door. Dad came to stop me, saying "Please, don't do this," but not longer under their influence, I left and went to stay at an apartment where two of Cynthia's friends lived. I didn't know them well, but I didn't care—I just want to get away. The day I moved in, dragging a ton of luggage with me, I walked into the elevator and guess who was there?—Reid White. Despite my rude behavior at the party, he greeted me with a smile and helped me bring my belongings up to my apartment. Amazingly, he lived in 9B and I, with my new roommates, in 6B. It seemed our marriage four years later was meant to be.

Soon after my meeting Reid, I got a job at NBC in their Program Analysis Department. When I went to NBC, I thought I was going to be doing think-work on whether the programs were answering the viewers' TV expectations, but I soon found that all I was doing was counting how many viewers watched each program; when they watched and were they happy with what they were watching.? I was so bored that I'd count the minutes until five o'clock and the bus home. By this time, I was sharing an apartment on E. 72nd street with a nice girl named Didi, who knew many New York celebrities who sometimes deigned to come to our unostentatious apartment. When we moved in, we had no idea that a live-in celebrity was just down our hall.

At this time, Reid lived across the street from our apartment and we dated all the time. If we'd had an argument at night, the next morning I'd look out of my window and there, on the sidewalk below, handsome Reid would be waiting for the bus to take him to work. He'd stand there, his hat tilted on his head like Fred Astaire and, seeing me, he'd start doing Astaire steps, winning me over with every one of his moves. I would laugh and be fully forgiving. Because he knew I adored cats, he gave me one. We called him Clawed Thornnail, named after the bandleader, Claude Thornhill, and I soon found out that Clawed was a serious explorer. One hot summer night, Clawed decided to get some fresh air and went out my window, walked along the outside ledge—nine floors above the street—until he found another open window. He, then, jumped in and landed right on top of a sleeping woman. Still looking for Clawed, Didi and I heard a knock on the door and there was a woman we did not know, holding Clawed. She looked at us, held him up, and said, "Your cat, I presume?" The woman was the famous Helene Hanff, author of the well-known book and its subsequent movie, "*84 Charing Cross Road.*"

Helene was not only famous and great fun, but also practical. One day, a shriveled old lady who lived in the building, walked down our hall to put a letter into the mail chute. Being very short and bent over, she couldn't reach her arm high enough to tip and drop her letter down the chute, so her hand got stuck in the slot. Everyone tried to help her and finally two firemen were called to fix the problem. It was obvious that freeing the old lady from the mail chute would require breaking the glass to extricate her hand and that would be dangerous. Just as this was about to happen, Helene came down the hall, carrying a bottle of Wesson Oil. She went to the chute, poured the Wesson oil over the lady's hand, and then slowly eased it out. Smart! However, now there are tons of oily letters at the bottom of the mail chute that would never reach their destinations.

Reid and I got to know Helene well (we're mentioned in her book, *Letters from New York*). We'd go to her apartment and she'd tell the real life stories of *84 Charing Cross Road* and we'd laugh and cry. We'd sing my family's funny songs to her and sometimes we'd go out for dinner. (Years later, when Reid and I returned from our home in San Francisco, she and some mutual friends came to meet us at the airport. There was Helene, carrying a shaker of martinis.)

After my stimulating job at NBC, I continued my hunt for the perfect job, where I wasn't just taking dictation, but maybe offering an idea or two. I found one working for the movie and TV Director, Herbert Bayard Swope, Jr., who produced a TV show called *The Race of the Week* from Aqueduct Racetrack. At my interview, he hinted that I might be able to do research on the horse owners which could spice up the show's commentary. Not surprisingly, this never happened and yet again, I was a personal secretary. However, the job was fun as Swope's connections with Hollywood brought many actors to the office. One part of my mindless duties was to arrange his weekly poker games that included Arlene Francis, one of the top radio show hosts of the day, and Tallulah Bankhead. I would call them and say, "The reading club is going to be held at John's house on Wednesday at 6:30." My famous boss didn't want the world to know of his poker nights. Another one of my boss's connections was hysterical Jonathan Winters, the comic and actor.

One day Jonathan came to the office to say "hello" to Herbert, hoping to be a part of one of Swope's projects. I was sitting at my typewriter and quickly offered to take him into Swope's office. Paying no attention to what I'd just said, he put his hands down into my typewriter carriage and whispered, "Type, 'I love you'." I pretended to type; he rolled his eyes and I took him into Swope's office. He was totally nuts and always funny.

This job did not last long for various reasons, one being *The Race of the Week* began to lose money and I was let go. When my boss told me I would have to be gone in three days I said, "Maids get three weeks notice!" He then told me to leave that very day. That night, in my apartment, furious, I got sufficiently bombed to call Swope's home. The phone was answered by someone I didn't know, seemingly a youngster who, when hearing my name, said

"Go shit in your hat!" Nice! Then I thought... wouldn't it be fun to try calling one of the world's most famous persons and see how far I could get? I picked Princess Margaret. Speaking in a heavy British accent, I got through to the operator at Buckingham Palace. I told her that I was Arlene Francis' secretary and wanted to talk with Princess Margaret about an upcoming program that would focus on her many charitable acts. I "ectually" reached the Princess's Private Secretary, at which point I knew it would be dangerous to go any further, and put the phone down. So much for *The Race of the Week*!

At this time, I met a super young woman named Helen Trimble. We'd met at a friend's wedding and during out small talk, we'd both cracked up over some hilarious joke and from that moment on, we became close friends. Because of this, we decided to room together and, having heard of a great apartment building on 79th Street, we went to see about renting an apartment but, sadly, found that the rule for living there was that you had to be a married couple. Clever as always, Helen and her boyfriend, Allan, pretended they were engaged and put money down for their apartment. Then they pretended to break up, and I took on the role of consoling friend. The manager felt sorry enough to allow a change in the rules and Helen and I became roommates along with my previous apartment-mate, Didi.

One night Didi and I were alone and decided to go to a movie. When we got home we were having tea when we noticed our radio was missing. We looked everywhere for it with no success. We went and told the building manager, who came back upstairs to check things out. When he opened our front closet door, there was the radio and all our coats on the floor. It seemed we'd been robbed and the robbers had been hiding in the closet all the time we were there, but when we'd left to see the manager they'd quietly slipped out the door. The police came and found a trail of muddy boot marks down the back stairs, but the robbers had escaped. After the hunt ended, the cops decided to give us a lesson about how robbers open locked doors. The cops pulled their credit cards out and went into the hall instructing us to lock the door. They yelled through the door, "It's pretty simple. You just insert the card, wiggle the edge a bit and—ta-da—it's open." Ta-da? They weren't able to open our door and we let them back in. Then, Didi took one of their cards; stood in the hall, inserted the card in the door, wiggled it and, yes—the door immediately opened. This wasn't hard for her as she'd learned the credit card trick before. The cops were clearly embarrassed so we ask them in for a drink. We had much fun and good talks.

That night we weren't treated as scared, incompetent women—we were treated like equals.

After my stint with *The Race of the Week*, I needed another job and the one I got resulted in even worse male treatment. This job was at the Goodson Todman Advertising Agency in the Seagram's building in Manhattan. My boss was a young, egotistical, advertising director who, when thinking about a letter he was about to dictate, would take a pencil from his pencil cup and shoot it across the desk, sometimes hitting me in the face. Granted, he shot me with the eraser end, but after a few days of this, I asked him to, "Please stop. This isn't funny anymore."

He told me, "Oh, that's just the way I concentrate."

I told him I couldn't work this way.

He looked at me and quietly said, "You're fired." I was glad, except where would I work next? The pencil-shooting took place during winter when the base of the massive fountain at the Seagram's Building was frozen. There were icicles hanging down, but I was ready. I'd written a note, signed it, and put the note in a sealed plastic bottle. I found a crack in the fountain's icy bottom and slipped the bottle far enough in so that it couldn't be seen. It was addressed to my boss and the note said, "Fuck you! I was going to quit anyway!" I knew that when spring came the ice would melt and my boss would receive my love letter. So much for Goodson Todman.

At this point I vowed I would never take a job that only required my fingers moving over a typewriter or a steno pad. This almost worked, as I became not only a personal secretary but an actual office manager.

Soon after working for the pencil-thrower, I ended up working for two famous, "pieces of work", doctors at a big-time hospital in the city. I was thrilled to have landed this job, especially as I'd loved the world of medicine since childhood. I had once told Mother that I wanted to be a nurse when I grew up. Mother had replied, "And empty bedpans all day? Never!" So, coming to be a glorified secretary in the world of medicine was not my dream, but near enough.

The two doctors I worked for were the heads of the Department of Endocrinology and secret doctors to President Kennedy. Quite often they went to Washington to tend to Kennedy's Addison's disease. These were secret meetings, as knowledge of his treatment might have led people to change their opinion of his ability to be an active president. The well-kept secret worked well.

When I went to be interviewed for my job, both doctors asked me how fast I could take shorthand. Even having had other jobs, I still wasn't an atomic stenographer, a fact I reluctantly admitted. The doctors looked at each other, smiled, and asked me to walk around the room. I didn't know why, but at this point, with my bank account nearly empty, I was willing to do just about anything for a job. So, as commanded, I circled the room in my mini-skirt with a lot of leg showing. Both men looked at each other, smiled broadly and said, "You're hired!" Today, I would have had reason to sue, but then I didn't care—it meant a salary.

Within a week, I realized I was working with pleasant people who had humor. I felt so at home that I made a sign that I hung at the top of the office door. In that I was working for two famous endocrinologists who treated glandular problems, the sign read, "The Gland Canyon Suite." Movie stars with sexual or more egregious malfunctions often came to see the doctors, so I got to wave at them and sometimes meet them. Soon, I got to know almost all the staff and doctors on our long floor. I also got to meet some not-so admirable persons. But one day, my job became "steno-graphic."

I was sitting alone in the office, typing away, when a young man in a white coat appeared at the door. His face was unfamiliar, but seeing the white coat, I assumed he was an intern. I looked at him and politely asked, "Can I help you?" I, immediately, knew he needed no help. He was jerking off, sowing his seed on the hallway floor. I screamed, "Get the fuck out!" and he turned and fled down the hall. I ran to my doctors next door, and yelled for help. One came out and I gasped out the fact that "some boy just came to the office and jerked off in front of me." My boss looked at me, raised one eyebrow and smiling said, "Laird, we all know you're in your twenties and still single ... you've just imagined it." I planted my feet directly in front of him, pointed to the office entrance and said, "Go take a slide!" It turned out that the young man was a patient in the adjoining psychiatric hospital and had found a way to sneak into our building. I had to identify him in a line-up but I only got to identify his face. Identifying another body part might have taken less time.

Can I help you?

Despite the Women's Liberation Movement, there were many men who wouldn't give up their opinion that women were—"just women." Even though my bosses were respectful to their office staff, one night one of them showed he had more respect for my body than for me—a person. That night, after he and I had been to an out-of-town lecture, he told me that before he took me back to my city apartment he had to check on some "work material" at his home. Soon we were in his living room having a cup of tea. It was fairly late at night and his wife and son were upstairs. We were sitting on the sofa and suddenly he was on top of me, trying to unbutton my blouse. I couldn't get away but, somehow, I was able to say something that made him laugh so hard that he bent backwards, allowing me to knee him in the crotch and in well-deserved pain, he rolled off the couch. I shouted loudly, "Call a taxi, now, or I'll call the police." Which he did. If I hadn't been able to joke, I would have been in serious trouble. On another night, while attending a hospital reception, my other boss—married with five kids—told me he'd leave his family if I'd marry him. I said "You gotta be kidding!" He told me he wasn't. I thanked him for the compliment and assured him that I'd be about as good a wife as I was a stenographer. He laughed and that was that.

Humor is important. One example of how humor breeds humor occurred during my hospital job on a slow afternoon when we office-workers were having our Tetley tea break. Quite often the strings on our tea bags would break, so on this afternoon, I decided to write a letter to the president of the company to let him know they had tea bag problems. As Tetley Tea is a British tea, I wrote my letter in a British accent hoping that my humor would lead them to "ectually" read my letter. I started it off by saying, "I'm teddibly sorry to be writing but I, and my afternoon tea-friends, are having a veddy hahd time using your tea begs." I got a letter back written by the vice president of the company. It was written in an English accent, telling me that they would "immedgetly look into the problem." He ended the letter wishing me many years of humor, plus he offered me a job.

My final New York job was being a—guess what?—at the J.M. Mathis advertising agency. All I can say is that what went on in this office made the show, *Mad Men*, seem like a kid's cartoon. Flirting was an expected part of a secretarial job. Despite the sound of the martini shaker often heard at lunchtime and the very mad men, it was an interesting job. I, actually, was allowed to give ideas for ad campaigns so, for the first time, my brain—not just my hands—were valued. This was my last job before getting married and the most important memory I have of this job was the day President Kennedy was killed. We were all at work and suddenly saw crowds of people huddled and crying across the street from our building. We soon learned the details and, unlike our usual behavior, cried and hugged each other for comfort, only, and closed the office.

When I worked at J.M. Mathis I had been dating Reid for four years. Because we were aware that our friends were curious (and often bored) with the fact that we weren't married, we sometimes hid out at downtown Hungarian restaurants to escape their questioning looks. During this long period of dating, I took a short break and started dating a drop-dead good looking French gynecologist. One night we were at a local bar with some other people and there, at the other end of the bar, was Reid White—checking up . (When Dad heard that I was dating a French gynecologist he said, "Laird. It's bad enough that he's a gynecologist—but *French!*") Finally, Reid got bored with Dating Without Decision, and moved to San Francisco and a new job.

Soon after Reid moved, my roommates, Helen and Judy, told me my four years of saying "I don't know" to Reid's proposals was an obvious sign that I needed a shrink. Helen knew of a psychiatrist, Dr. Silvia Fine, and on her advice, I went to Dr. Fine for help. Miss Fine, as her patients called her, was humorous and each time I saw her she'd ask "How are you, Laird?" to which I'd answer, "I'm fine" and then she'd say, "No! *I'm* Fine!" We'd howl with laughter and then start the session. During one of my sessions, I told her about my childhood experience with the mummy in the Boston Museum of Natural History resulting in my dream of the mummy at the bottom of my bed. A few nights after that appointment I had a dream and when I told her about it, her eyebrows hit the ceiling. In the dream, I was a bride going down the aisle of a church to be married before the altar. I was dressed in a body-hugging bridal gown made of thin, white material wrapped round and round my body. Miss Fine said she'd never had an easier diagnosis. The dream clearly showed that, for me, the thought of marriage, and being a bride and then a "Mummy", harkened back to my memories of my own mother's lack of maternal warmth and her questionable marriage. Deep down I feared that marriage might be a skeleton death. She assured me that what I saw back then, didn't mean that I had to experience it that way in my own life. When I got home, I told Judy, "I'm ready," and called Reid's work number. When he picked up the phone I gasped, "I want to marry you!" and in a very business-like voice Reid replied, "Thank you for calling, Mr. Jones. I'm in a business meeting right now, but will get back to you with the information as soon as I can." When his meeting was over he ran downstairs to a pay phone and called me. In two minutes we were engaged! Now, I'd landed a job where I'd work alongside a loveable—"piece of work."

We take the cake!

12 AISLE DO IT!

When I was at boarding school, my friends and I got together one night and told each other things we would never do. I told them I would never marry a southerner (like Mother), a Yalie (a snob), a banker (a bore), or drive a station wagon (too suburban). I ended up with all four!

Reid and I were engaged on January 15, 1964 and

married on the twenty-ninth of February— Leap Year Day—the only day when the church was available. As our engagement only lasted forty five days, everyone thought I was pregnant—tsk! tsk!

Within one day of hearing the news of my engagement, Mother was making wedding plans. My wedding was to be as glorious as hers had been and, of course, my getting a wedding dress was at the top of her list. I'd always had the vision of being married at Green Pastures, or somewhere in the country. I pictured a casual wedding and reception. I'd wear a simple, short wedding dress but, with Mother at the helm, I was not going to sail into marriage that way—I was going to sail in on the Queen Mary.

As for pre-marriage and being engaged, there was one incident that embodied Mother's views. It was also an incident that made us Trowbridge kids realize that, despite our differences, we were alike. Mother, on one occasion, may have been the naughty wife, but God forbid, any of *us* should be naughty, and definitely not before marriage! "Sex" was a word not to be spoken until the bridal gown was on its trip back from "I do."

A few months before my wedding, Mother had suffered badly from the flu and was bedridden in her New York apartment. Worried about her health, Anne, Sal, Rob and I went to see her. I remember the four of us were sitting across from her bed, making small talk. Mother was propped up on her pillow, her face pale and the ever-present cigarette resting right there in her ashtray. For some reason, the conversation turned to Sal's wedding, years back. Mother pulled herself up a bit and, looking at us, croaked, "I've always been so proud of my children having behaved ... properly ... before marriage." In one motion, all of our heads dropped and silence rang throughout the room.

But now, it was time to get the prescribed virginal wedding dress. As my job at J.M. Mathis only allowed me a forty-five-minute lunch, I quickly rushed to Bloomingdales to find the first item on Mother's list: the dress. Any dress. The veil would be Mother's delicate one made of embroidered lace. When I got to Bloomingdales, I rushed to the bridal department; flipped through a mass of white dresses hanging on a rack and, finally, found a simple one with short sleeves and a scoop neck. I sat down with the dress on my lap and waited for help. Suddenly, I saw a young woman dressed in a fairytale satin wedding dress, standing with her mother who was talking to a saleswoman. They were in front of a large mirror and the young girl kept turning around to see how the dress looked from all angles. Her mother was "ooing" and "aaaaing" with delight, telling her she looked "gworrrgeous," and the saleswoman was standing with her hand over her mouth, obviously trying not to laugh. I was holding my hand over my mouth, too, as the young girl's stomach looked like a huge basket ball about to drop through the hoop. She was very, very pregnant—before marriage—tsk, tsk!

I bought my dress in twenty minutes and to this day, it lies embalmed in an airtight box in the attic. However, I look at it almost every day, not upstairs, but when doing the laundry. On the wall, next to our washing machine, is a dramatically absurd wedding picture of me, taken by the well-known society photographer, J.T. Winbourne, (hired by Mother and paid for by Cousin Sue.) In the picture, I'm standing in the dress; mother's veil hangs down and on my face is a shy, virginal look. I am looking down to my hand that holds a limp wedding bouquet; its lovely flowers bashfully facing the floor. At the bottom of the photograph I've written: "Mother, I'd rather do it myself!!"

Our wedding was a very classy New York affair with the service at All Saint's Church and a huge reception at a snappy address in a five-star hotel. As Dad wanted to walk me down the aisle, Uncle George happily agreed to perform the ceremony. A week before the wedding, Reid and I had met with him at his home. This "meeting with the minister," was one required by the church. The minister and engaged couple must talk about factors that make for a happy marriage. We were told by Dad that the subjects of discussion would include topics such as "an understanding of each other's needs"; the bride and groom's relations with each other's parents, etc. All of the prerequisites for a good marriage were numbered on the list of topics.

On the day of our meeting, we were sitting with Uncle George, going through the list of questions, when suddenly he had to leave the room to answer the phone. Reid and I quickly looked at the list and, to our horror, found that No. 9 was entitled —"Sex"! We'd already hit No. 7. We heard Uncle George returning and quickly put the list in its place, trying to look tranquil. Then we waited for what seemed hours until George finished No. 8. To our heaven-sent joy, he skipped No. 9 and went right to 10 without blinking an eye. Uncle George was, clearly— "with-it."

Uncle George also lightened up the actual marriage ceremony. At that time in the sixties the word "obey" was still included in the marriage vows, but when he came to the vow of "love and obey," he said "to love," then paused for a notable amount of time and whispered loudly enough for the first row of guests to hear: "I think we'll skip 'obey.'" The bride, the groom, and the wedding guests had a good laugh.

The wedding reception was a big, beautiful success, except that I had a bad cold and felt terrible. Despite this, I smiled, laughed with my matron of honor, Helen, and my bridesmaids. I did all the right things a happy bride should do, but afterwards, when we went to the Plaza Hotel for our first married night together, I collapsed on the bed with a nose as stuffed as a Christmas stocking. We called the front desk and asked for some nose spray to be sent to the room. After a few moments, there was a knock on the door and in came the bellboy with a small bottle of something on a silver tray. It was a bottle of mint mouthwash. The front desk obviously had assumed that any order from the bridal suite must have something to do with lovemaking, in this instance, maybe bad breath. Without mint in the mouth, lovemaking would be sour—not sweet.

The day after our marriage we left for our honeymoon at a resort in the Bahamas. We took a British Overseas Airways Corporation (BOAC) flight and hating to fly, I was clutching Reid's hand as we took off. Quite suddenly the plane's tail hit the tarmac and we shot up at a terrifying speed. The rest of the flight was normal but, from then on, I referred to BOAC as "Britain's Oldest Air Corpse."

The "resort" was right on a beautiful beach, but our

travel agent had neglected to tell us that the whole place was old and run down. The picture she'd showed us had been taken years before. Grass was growing out of the tennis court and the buildings needed paint. One afternoon, when we were doing what all honeymooners do, the door opened and in shuffled a large maid with a mop. In a heavy, swinging Bahamian accent she said, "Don't mine me ... I got five of dem children." After a week sitting on the beach and in the bar, we left for San Francisco, our new life and, soon, my new and most challenging job—that of being the wife of a really nice man.

Our first home was on Telegraph Hill where we rented a luxurious...one-bedroom apartment. I was filled with angst about being a married woman. Would I be stuck as the "little wife," expected to clean, cook, and enjoy being alone while Reid was working at the Bank of California? The master bedroom (the only bedroom), was so cramped that the open door hit the bed and, not wanting to be confined to this apartment and needing money, I found a job at a placement agency where I helped young women find work in many types of employment—not just secretarial.

In 1965, I became pregnant. It was time to move and so we moved to a larger, lovely apartment that looked out to a beautiful courtyard. Our daughter, Emilie was born on April Fool's Day—hardly appropriate for her as she's very, very smart. It was not an easy birth. When she finally emerged, she looked like an alien from Mars who'd just been in a slug fight. There were two hematomas on either side of her head, making her not just an alien, but a Disney Mouseketeer, and her nose was bent straight down. It turned out that, during delivery, she'd done a figure eight with the umbilical cord. If it hadn't been for my talented doctor, she would have died. When he lifted her up for me to see, he said, "Laird, I've delivered a thousand babies and this is the ugliest I've ever seen ... but she'll be beautiful."

Along with the hematomas, Emilie had colic. Each evening she would scream for what seemed forever. It was very hard for us, as well as her, but one night, exactly three months past her birth, we suddenly realized something was wrong. The apartment was quiet. Worried that the silence meant something bad had happened, we ran into her room and there she lay, her hematomas gone, her face baby-pink and her little body peacefully asleep. My doctor had been right—she was beautiful—and still is.

Within the next few months, Reid found a new banking job back in Manhattan and it was time to leave California. The day we left, a taxi was waiting below to take us to the airport. Emilie was ready to go and we were in our bedroom checking to see if we'd packed everything. For the last time, I looked out our wide bedroom sliding door that faced the courtyard. There, across from our door was Sandy, an annoying apartment-neighbor, washing dishes at her sink. Sandy was a nosy person who spent most of her days casing out people from her kitchen window or her open apartment door. Her main activity was making sure she knew where all her neighbors were at every moment and she constantly checked out our bedroom. Wanting to say a final "goodbye" to Sandy, I told Reid how I wanted to say it. Reid nodded; lowered his pants; turned around and stood behind our wide curtains. I, then, drew the curtains back and Reid "mooned" her. Immediately, we grabbed Emilie, ran to our waiting taxi and in a flash—we were gone.

Due to pressure in her ears, Emilie began screaming as soon as we took off in the plane and Reid, embarrassed and wanting to escape the racket, went down the aisle, and, with drink in hand, flirted with the stewardess. I waved him back to keep me company while Emilie cried from pain.

When we landed at the airport in Newark, New Jersey, I burst into tears of relief. The stewardess said, "I've seen

people cry at hundreds of airports—but never at Newark!"
Newark Airport was not known for its beauty but I was
thrilled to land there. It meant we were on the East Coast
again, near to our families and on our way to live in
Princeton, New Jersey, the source of much Trowbridge
family history.

Our second daughter, Gillian, luckily emerged without
trauma and looked like a regular, adorable baby. Reid and I
spent most of our time cuddling and watching our children
as if we'd never seen children before. It was hard to believe
that these sweet beings were actually ours. Working in
New York, Reid didn't get home until seven thirty, so
during the week he only had time to peek at them sleeping.
Eventually he and his talented friend, Steve Fillo, started
their own business and our parental life became a bit more
normal. During those early years, I'd look at my daughter's
faces and wonder about their futures. As a writer, I'm
thrilled that both of them turned out to be writers and
teachers, both with advanced degrees and both authors.
Gillian became an associate professor of contemporary
poetry at the University of Michigan, and Emilie, a writer
and part-time teacher in North Carolina. Between the two
of them, we have three outstanding, healthy grandchildren
with whom I am never bored.

Gillian and Emilie

I'll never forget a day when I was visiting Gillian at her home in Michigan. She, her husband, Jamie, and Reid and I were madly chatting in the living room while her two children raced around playing a game. I was looking out of the window and suddenly I felt two arms around my legs. I looked down and there was Henry, my four-year-old grandson, hugging me, his cheek against my waist. Then, I heard him say, "Grandma Laird, I love you more than I can

say." Those words meant everything to me. When I'm feeling low, I think of them, and I smile inside and out.

Our life in Princeton was one of bringing up our children, meeting new and lasting friends and being involved with entertainment. The children were the most important part of our lives, the friends were our supporters, and the entertainment was a busy, enormously fun sidebar. We spent around ten years singing in a jazz group that, formally, was called The Witherspooners, but known by us as The Private Parts.

The Private Parts

Our director, Roo Brown, was extremely talented and the numbers we sang were jazzy. We were good and did some singing in other states but, finally, the group disbanded.

Two years before the Private Parts closed down we had become involved with The Inn Cabaret which took place at the prominent Nassau Inn in Princeton. Some members of our singing group were part of the show and it was directed by a very talented young man, Dan Berkowitz, who to this day, is still in the entertainment business. Reid sang and I wrote comedy skits and parodies. One of my favorite memories is that of coming into the entryway of the inn and seeing a sign that said, "Another number by Laird White." For me that sign was a milestone, marking how music and humor had become my signature. Apparently, Laird White could make people laugh.

Even though I was now Laird White, I was still, Laird Trowbridge—child of the crazy family that, whenever possible, made humor their main meal. Now, a thousand years later, Laird Trowbridge White still finds that a fun experience, a humorous remark or thought can be a life raft in this ever-changing ocean of life.

Reid Roman through a cabaret skit

13 LAUGH INSURANCE

"A day without humor is a day wasted."
~ Charlie Chaplin

Reid and I have been married for eons and, like any married couple, we've had our ups and downs. His work, his bike, and his kayak keep him going. My writing, whether it be serious poetry, this piece, or my mystery to come—have helped keep me going. Our love for our children and friends are our backbone for our lasting marriage. But the tendons that help hold that backbone in line come from our "tendoncy" (sorry!) to call on humor for support.

For me, humor is a hat that one can put on when necessary. It can be the small cap of a pun, or as blatantly brimmed as burlesque. It cannot alleviate tragedy, but when it provides even a smile of happiness to another person, it creates happiness for oneself.

What a GREAT joke!

If, when walking down the street, you smile at someone coming toward you, most often they will smile back, but, usually, you have to do it first. If you are able to find something positive in the non-positives of life you will be buoyed up. You will have Laugh Insurance and this will help you withstand many of life's difficulties.

My Laugh Insurance was born from our family, "speaking in tunes." Singing funny songs was the glue that held us together. Mother, who could only croak through her cigarette smoke, finally took up the accordion which she played about as well as a three- year- old, but it didn't matter— it gave her a chance to be a sometimes member of the Singing Trowbridges. We weren't the Trapp Family Singers, of the movie *"The Sound of Music:"*, we were just five hams, singing in our Green Pastures kitchen and barn; on car trips and at people's dinner parties, but we did it well. Rob, our baritone, liked to poke fun and dubbed us The Crapp Family Singers.

The Crapp Family singers

Although we sang normal songs like "Row Row Row Your Boat," our favorites were clever parodies my father had learned years before from his friend, Stacy Holmes. Stacy had attended the Boston Latin School in the '20s and one of his assignments had been to translate a popular song into Latin. Wanting to astound his teacher, he decided to use the Tin Pan Alley hit, "I'm Forever Blowing Bubbles," and make it suitable for entertaining Nero and the lions on a coliseum afternoon in Rome. What we sang began something like this: "Semper faciens qui bublos,/ pulcras bublos in aerae" (I'm forever blowing bubbles/ pretty bubbles in the air). A few years ago I sang it at a dinner party and a Latin teacher happened to be sitting across from me. When I finished the song, she stared at me, raised one eyebrow and said, ... "sort of." It didn't matter. People laughed.

Quite a few of our songs were a wee bit off-color, such as, "It's The Wrong Thing to Tickle Mary" or, "I'm the Only Man in The World Who Can Take a Biscuit Apart" but my family-favorite is one called, "My Old Man's Liver"—a takeoff of *"Ole Man River."* Daddy, drink in hand, would sing it beautifully and it reeked of sincere feeling.

My old man's liver,
my old man's liver,
he just keeps drinkin'
"till he gets stinkin'.
My old man's liver,
It just keeps floatin' ... along.

He drinks whiskey
and he drinks brandy,
in fact—he swallows,
whatever's handy.
My old man's liver,
it just keeps floatin'... along.

It continues with its drinking theme and at some dinner parties, Reid sings it in his warm baritone voice. When Dad turned fifty, Sally put all our songs into a book entitled the Trowbridge Family Song Book. She'd sectioned the types of songs with page-tabs and one of them was tagged "NPP"—a title mother had given those off-color songs. "NPP" stood for "Non-Parish Picnic," songs totally inappropriate for an occasion such as church get-togethers. This was a hard order for my father, as he was an unrestrained performer and adored breaking down social barriers. As the "fellowship of man" was his source of the Holy Spirit, the sound of people laughing in fellowship of any kind, was part of his religion. Sadly, I am the only one left in my immediate family, but I have twelve nieces and nephews with whom I keep in contact. Most of them know some of the old funny songs and when we get together, we sing and howl with laughter. This practice has now been passed down through four generations.

An example of this is when my granddaughter, Maddie, was only five and learned a "Trowbridge Song." One summer day, she and her Aunt Gillian, had to sit for a long time in Gilly's car waiting for an inspection on their way to Nantucket. While waiting, Gilly sang one of our songs and Maddie repeatedly asked her to sing it, again and again. We learned about this when we were all at a family reunion in Newport, Rhode Island. Our daughters and children were there along with many of our nieces and nephews and we all met at a local restaurant to have lunch. We had two long tables on a balcony on the upper floor, but there were other patrons spread throughout the restaurant. As we were waiting for our meal to arrive, someone started singing one of our family songs and we all joined in. Then, Gilly turned to Maddie and said, "Maddie, would you like to sing your song?" Suddenly Maddie, in a surprisingly strong, clear voice, started singing the "Biscuit Song."

"I'm the only man in the world
who can take a biscuit apart,
and put it back together again.

If you don't believe what I'm sayin',
ask the lady where I'm stayin'...
If I does, or if I don't.

Rudy Valentino had a lot of fun.
but what he did to women,
I can do to a bun.

I'm the only man in the world
who can take a biscuit apart
And put it back together...again!,
  (not even lose a crumb...)
And put it back together...again!

While singing, Maddie smiled a sly smile and, enticingly, rolled her eyes. She had every word down pat—and it was all on tune. The people at the other tables were in hysterics and burst into applause. Maddie didn't expect this. After all, wasn't it just a regular old song about a biscuit?

When in a scary situation, humor can be a savior; sometimes even in the case of medical scares. One day, my doctor discovered that I had no pulse in my left leg and would need a stent to prevent a serious arterial blockage. I was terrified.

When would the big blow to the heart come? Where would the funeral take place? When the day of surgery arrived, I was put on a gurney and four medical assistants began wheeling me down to the operating room. They were deadly quiet which scared me to death. To death? Yes. I was certainly going die.

As we rolled down the hall into surgery, one of the medical assistants gave me a pre-op shot to calm me down. It didn't calm me down—it pumped me up— and suddenly I started singing a parody song I'd written when Reid and I were active with the Princeton Cabaret. The song was one I wrote for a convention of surgeons. (Knowing many of them would come to the cabaret, I decided to "doctor up" the show.)

The skit opens with a patient on a gurney being wheeled on stage. Four surgeons, dressed in surgical greens and masks, are standing at attention, waiting. They are armed with huge carving knives. The head surgeon speaks, encouraging his young surgical team—about to begin their first real surgery—to do their very best. He asks them to bow their heads and say the Surgeon's Prayer. There is a roll of drums with a cymbal finish. And then, to the tune of *"Another Opening, Another Show"* they sing what I sang to the two masked men wheeling me toward my death.

Another openin', another "Joe,"
Take out his spleen...
NO! His kidneys go!
A time for surgeons to make some dough.
Another openin' of another Joe.

Another job, Gee, I hope it's fast!
I've got a golf game at quarter past.
Don't leave the sponge in, it's bound to show.
Another openin' of another Joe.

Bridge:

Four years you rehearse and rehearse;
three years you spend screwing some nurse.
One year—time to get a good wife—
then out of the hat—it's that First Big Knife!

Last verse:

The overture is about to start,
Is that his liver? NO! That's his heart!
Well, take out SOMETHING, he'll never know!
Another openin' of another openin'—
of An..oth...er...Joe!

I only got through the first verse but the two medical assistants, now roaring with laughter said, "Laird, be quiet!" and then gave me a shot to shut me up. My thought had been that if I don't make it through the surgery, at least I'll have died laughing.

One of the biggest laughs at our cabaret came from a parody I wrote based on the old song, "On The Road To Mandalay". This song had been based on Kipling's poem and Frank Sinatra did *his* parody of it in the late fifties. My parody was born on a Saturday night at a boring cocktail party in Princeton.

That night, I was sitting beside one of Princeton's "old guard", a pillar of the community— famous for his deep, rich singing voice. We were talking about an upcoming cabaret performance and suddenly he said, "You know...I would *love* to sing in one of Cabaret's performances." Being polite, I asked him what song he'd like to sing and he replied, "Oh. 'On Road To Mandalay!' It's my *favorite* song." I told him that "On The Road..." wasn't a very funny song and that our whole show was designed to be humorous. I then patted his hand and said, "I'll do what I can do". That night I went home and wrote the following. We had it set up so that he was seated in the back of, what looked like an old roadster, singing with gusto while a chauffeur, played by Dan Berkowitz, who sat behind the wheel. (This parody became a cabaret favorite and Reid and I still sing it at the drop of anyone's hat. I named it, "On The Road To *Oyster* Bay":

On The Road To Oyster Bay

Verse:

Seven miles past Locust Valley,
Driving Eastward by the sea.
Is the place I spent my childhood,
And it means the world to me!

Roll the window down, please, Bentley,
I should like to smell the spray,
Drive me back, you British chauffeur,
Drive me back to Oyster Bay!...

Chorus:

On... the road to Oyster Bay.
Where the Old Guard swim and play.
You can hear their ice-cubes tinkling
In Vermouth and Tangueray.

On the road to Oyster Bay,
We have netball and croquet,
And the dawn comes up like thunder
From New Haven, 'cross the bay.

2nd Verse:

Never fly me to Nantucket.
Never drive me to Cape cod.
You may only drive me, Bentley,
to the Summa Place of god!

238

For, if there had been no Eden,
Nor a heavenly place to stay...
God, I'm sure.. would have vacationed,
Every year at Oyster Bay...

Chorus:

On the road to Oyster Bay,
Mummy's waiting at the quay.
Look! She's wearing her new Lilly,
that she bought in Saint-Tropez!

On the road to Oyster Bay,
Where the Summa People Play,
And the yawns come up like thunder...
From the BOREDOM OF... THE DAY!

Humor can also help turn anger into comedy as it did one night at our home in Princeton. A neighbor, who lived down the street in a mansion, had been mean to Emilie and Gillian and very cold to us. One day Emilie and Gillian had taken a walk down our country road and wandered onto the neighbor's lawn to stare in awe at the mansion. Mr. Mansion came out and yelled, "Get out! This is private property! Don't ever trespass again!" This didn't surprise us. When we'd just moved into our new house, we'd asked Mr. Mansion and his wife over for a Sunday cup of tea. The Mansions had declined, not because they were busy, but because Mr. Mansion told us, "We're sort of loners over here, but thanks anyway." After these two happenings, Mr. Mansion was on our blacklist and during the weekend after he had been mean to the kids, we retaliated, not with meanness, but hilarious fun inspired by—a frog.

Next to our little stone house was a teeny swimming pool, bordered by deep woods. The pool had become home for a very large frog whom we'd named Owen. One hot night, Owen was croaking so loudly that we couldn't sleep. Reid decided to get the pool scoop and flip Owen out of the pool and into the woods. Reid was naked when he went out and, after finally locating Owen, tossed him way out from the pool but, wanting his swim, Owen came hopping back. Reid said, "We've got to rid of him!" and thinking he was going to kill Owen, I ran out and screamed, "Don't kill him! He's Owen!" We looked at each other and agreed that we had to move Owen far away, but to where? You, of course, know where!

Nodding to each other, Reid grabbed Owen by the legs and we walked to our car. Reid, stark naked, got onto the back seat with Owen hanging between his knees. I got in the front seat to drive, my sweaty nightgown clinging to my body, and we drove down the road. I kept praying that the cops wouldn't catch us, as how would we explain a nude man holding a huge frog with its legs hanging between the man's...not-so-private-parts. When we reached the mansion, we took Owen out of the car, and tiptoeing onto Mr. Mansion's front lawn, set him free. Owen was thrilled with his new home and went happily hopping and croaking toward Mr. Mansion's massive pool. We couldn't have found a better gift for our friendly neighbor down the street. Deep dislike had been conquered by humor.

Humor can also lessen the stink of politics. These days, whatever your leanings are, it's clear that politics have become crazy and uncontrollable. My way of battling political insanity is to write ditties that make certain situations tolerable. I wrote one at the time of the 2008 presidential primary. It's sung to Dvorak's Humoresque.

Gentlemen will please refrain
from flushing women down the drain,
by preaching that a rape's an Act of God.

Hillary, when she's the Prez-
will be applauded when she sez.
"You rape? I'll take an axe—to your pea-pod!

(And...In April of 2016, the following—
to "Humpty Dumpty"):

Trumpty, Dumpty wanted a wall,
Trumpty, Dumpty shit over all.
May all of his bigotry, insults and phlegm,
put Trumpty Dump—in a Mexican pen!

The most important thing humor can do—and it did for me—is to save a life. One day, I was doing my weekly volunteer work for a suicide prevention group in Princeton. My job was to answer the phone, talk to the suicidal person who'd called, and give them the number of an appropriate therapist for help. What I did was only the first step in this scary process as, if needed, the police would be contacted to do whatever was necessary. One day I got a call from a woman who was talking in a low voice and threatening to kill herself. Her husband had left her and taken her two children, and she had no money. She was rambling on and on, and clearly drunk, so I interrupted her by yelling, "Have you heard this one?"

Startled by my sudden, unusual question she said, "What?" and I quickly told her a joke.

She started to laugh and I interrupted by saying, "See, if you're dead—you can't laugh!"

There was a moment of silence and then she whispered, "Yah. You're right."

I got her address and soon the help was on the way. I kept

talking to her until I could hear the cops yelling, "Help is here!" at her door. A laugh had helped save her life.

Doctor Humor—as I call it—has protected me from old fears that were born during my childhood. If unable to stop my brain, crammed with scary thoughts, I think of a funny song I might write and then I'm relaxed. During the day I work on my writing— often my poetry. Generally, my poems are serious, but some are not. In 1978 on the anniversary of Ogden Nash's birthday, the subject of cloning was hot. I couldn't sleep so I got my yellow pad and wrote a funny one. That night I had a great sleep!

Come Back, Ogden, You're Wanted on the Clone

What used to be "au naturel"
for rabbits in the Dingly Dell
to do, will soon be done alone,
in some drab lab to make … a clone.
           (everyone's agog—
           they've already done a frog!)

If more of you is what you wish,
get out your freshman petri dish.
A hank of hair, a rag, a bone,
"I'd like you to meet my son … the clone."
           (Want a daughter?
           add sugar and water!)

But, if I clone myself this week,
how do I know I'm at my peak?
Two weeks from now it might be better-a
to make myself, et cet, et cetera.
                    (Just to spite 'em
                    I'll make myself ad infinitum).

I find this process so depressing,
To multiply without undressing.
To make a him a her a ms.,
without, at least, a goodnight ks.
                    (this sterile path to progeny…
                    how stogeny!)

Finally, one question:
if I have sinus, will my clone have congestion?
And … after the cloning is over and done
with,who, in the HELL did I have any fun with?

P.S. (and I promise this is it)
I hope you scientists will quit,
for we prefer our present position
of reproducing by the sin of emission.

As I grow older, I like to make fun of the inevitable negatives
of aging, so a few years ago I wrote the following parody of
"The Continental"— a song from *"The Gay Divorcee,"* a
movie starring Ginger Rogers and Fred Astaire:

The Incontinental

It's alimental,
incontinental.
It's when those valves work...
now and then by chance.
Don't be judgmental,
incontinental,
Someday you, too, will poo poo
in your pants.

First incidental
inconsequential,
It happens when you sneeze,
 or blow your nose or dance.
It isn't mental,
It accidental,
But face it...baby,
you've peed in your pants!

Bridge:

Don't risk fancy dancing...
Be extra gentle... Incontinental!

Tsk! Tsk! on romancing...
Let sex be mental... Incontinental!

Ending:

It's all downhill from here, my friends.
There's nothing we old farts can do when we're old
but wear *two* "Depends".
So, piss... in those pant-things.
Your ali-ment-tary canal is shot,
You can't eat lentils... anything that's hot,
Or else you'll spend your whole life on the pot—
The End!

As crazy as it may seem, I have even written a humorous song for my memorial service. I've done this for two reasons; the main one being that I want people to remember me with a smile; the second being that if I smile now, I'll have ammunition against the fear of then. I don't expect anyone will choose to sing the song, but it's not only a funny one about dying— it's also one about living. . It is a take-off of the song *"Dancing Cheek to Cheek"* from the show *Puttin' on the Ritz."* I call it "Whatevah"—as I have no certainty of what, if anything, is beyond.

Whatevah

Heaven. Can't be heaven.
I can't see a goddamn thing... except my feet!
Do they make us go around here, incomplete?
Or is this that Other Place,
The one with heat?

Heaven? This ain't heaven.
'Cuz I have no mouth, no arms, no legs,...... no teeth!
I can't whistle, I can't chew, or take a leak.
But, I'm hearing music–
Look! I'm dancing!... Neat!

Bridge:

If you're low, pick up... go dancing!
Put your arms around your sweet.
When life gets dark.
stroll through a park
and hear the birdies tweet.

Last verse:

Heaven? Bet on seven.
Roll those dice and hit that jackpot at its peak!
But if you don't win, - well, try a spin, next week.
In the meantime, go out dancing— cheek to cheek.

I believe humor is inherent and lies in all of us—waiting to be birthed. As proof, think of newborn babies who, six months after birth, can instinctively smile at the wiggle of someone's finger. No, Dr. humor can't heal the tragedies in our world or the world out there, but if allowed, he can help open an umbrella to protect us from the inevitable downpours in life. I believe that a chuckle lies snuggled up in all of us and, if let out to play, will help us live happier lives. I was lucky. I learned the protective and delightful benefits of humor at a young age and have coddled them ever since. I pray it will be my friend who sits by my side—and yours—until the very end. Hopefully, it will create many "five star Sundays" for us all, while helping us survive those inevitable "two star Mondays."

ABOUT THE AUTHOR

Laird White has been a writer of poetry, prose and comedy material since early on in life. Her book of poetry, "Barefoot Walking" was published two years ago. Having grown up in a (mostly) humorous family she has used the walking stick of humor to get her through life. Laird attended Mt. Holyoke College where she majored in English and philosophy. She now lives in Lenox, Massachusetts. Her family and her writing are her favorite companions.

Made in the USA
Charleston, SC
07 February 2017